Buddhist Ethics
in
Impermanence

Emerging Perceptions in Buddhist Studies
(ISSN 0971-9512)

1-2. An Encyclopaedia of Buddhist Deities, Demigods, Godlings, Saints & Demons — with Special Focus on Iconographic Attributes; by Fredrick W. Bunce. 2 Vols. (ISBN 81-246-0020-1; set)

3. Buddhism in Karnataka; by R.C. Hiremath; with a foreword by H.H. the Dalai Lama (ISBN 81-246-0013-9)

4-5. Pāli Language and Literature: A Systematic Survey and Historical Study; by Kanai Lal Hazra. 2 Vols. (ISBN 81-246-0004-X; set)

6. Maṇḍala and Landscape; by A.W. Macdonald (ISBN 81-246-0060-0)

7. The Future Buddha Maitreya: An Iconological Study; by Inchang Kim (ISBN 81-246-0082-1)

8. Absence of the Buddha Image in Early Buddhist Art; by Kanoko Tanaka (ISBN 81-246-0090-2)

9. A Few Facts About Buddhism; by Gunnar Gällmo (ISBN 81-246-0099-6)

10. Buddhist Theory of Meaning and Literary Analysis; by Rajnish K. Mishra (ISBN 81-246-0118-6)

11. Buddhism as/in Performance; Analysis of Meditation and Theatrical Practice; by David E.R. George (ISBN 81-246-0123-2)

12. Buddhist Tantra and Buddhist Art; by T.N. Mishra (ISBN 81-246-0141-0)

13. Buddhist Art in India and Sri Lanka: 3rd Century BC to 6th Century AD — A Critical Study; by Virender Kumar Dabral (ISBN 81-246-0162-3)

14. The Tibetan Iconography of Buddhas, Bodhisattvas and Other Deities — A Unique Pantheon; by Lokesh Chandra & Fredrick W. Bunce (ISBN 81-246-0178-X)

15. The Dalai Lamas — The Institution and Its History by Ardy Verhaegen; (ISBN 81-246-0202-6)

16. The Tibetan Tāntric Vision; by Krishna Ghosh Della Santina (ISBN 81-246-0227-1)

17. The Buddhist Art of Kauśāmbī; by Aruna Tripathi: From 300 BC to AD 550 (ISBN 81-246-0226-3)

18. Mahāmudrā & Atiyoga; by Giuseppe Baroetto; Translated from Italian into English by Andrew Lukianowicz (ISBN 81-246-0322-7)

19. Theravāda Buddhist Devotionalism in Ceylon, Burma and Thailand; by V.V.S. Saibaba (ISBN 81-246-0327-8)

20. Faith and Devotion in Theravāda Buddhism; by V.V.S. Saibaba (ISBN 81-246-0329-4)

21. Sects in Tibetan Buddhism — Comparison of Practices Between Gelugpa and Nyingmapa Sects; by Vijay Kumar Singh (ISBN-81-246-0330-8)

22. Emptiness and Becoming — Integrating Mādhyamika Buddhism and Process Philosophy; by Peter Paul Kakol (ISBN 81-246-0519-6)

Emerging Perceptions in Buddhist Studies, no. 23

Buddhist Ethics in Impermanence

M.V. Ram Kumar Ratnam
K. Srinivas

D.K. Printworld (P) Ltd.
Publishers of Indian Traditions

Cataloging in Publication Data — DK
[Courtesy: D.K. Agencies (P) Ltd. <docinfo@dkagencies.com>]

Ram Kumar Ratnam, M.V., 1956-
Buddhist ethics in impermanence / M.V. Ram Kumar Ratnam, K. Srinivas.

p. cm. — (Emerging perceptions in Buddhist studies ; no. 23)
Includes bibliographical references (p.) and index.
ISBN 13: 9788124605622
ISBN 10: 8124605629

1. Impermanence (Buddhism) 2. Buddhist ethics. I. Srinivas, K. (Kunchapudi), 1955-, joint author. II. Title. III. Series: Emerging perceptions in Buddhist studies ; no. 23.

DDC 294.35 22

First published in India, 2011
ISBN 13: 978-81-246-0562-2 (HB) ISBN 10: 81-246-0562-9

Published and printed by:
D.K. Printworld (P) Ltd.
Regd. office : *'Srikunj,'* F-52, Bali Nagar
Ramesh Nagar Metro Station
New Delhi – 110 015
Phones : (011) 2545 3975; 2546 6019; *Fax* : (011) 2546 5926
E-mail: indology@dkprintworld.com
Web: www.dkprintworld.com

To

Our Kalyanamitta

Professor C. Ramaiah

Formerly, Professor & Head, Department of Philosophy,
Sri Venkateswara University, Tirupati

Preface

THE present work only serves as a good introduction to those who are interested in getting themselves acquainted with the fundamental ethical precepts of Buddhism. This work is neither elementary nor highly advanced treatise on Buddhist ethics. True to the Buddhist ideal, we chose the middle path in writing this book. Lot of insightful research was done in the past, and is being done now in this field by the outstanding Buddhist scholars both in the Orient and the Occident. A list of such important works is presented in the select bibliography for the benefit of those who would like to get into the deeper structures of Buddhist ethics. An exhaustive study of Buddhist ethics may not be possible in one single life, for it is an ocean by itself. We only picked up some pebbles that lie on the shores of this ocean. The modern man is so busy with his day-to-day personal and social responsibilities. He may not find enough time to spare to go through in detail these highly technical and insightful research works on Buddhist ethics. He looks for something that gives him immediate solace to his mental stress and satisfaction to his intellectual urge. This work certainly serves the purpose for such individuals. At the same time, the present work has its own academic worth, for it tries to show the relevance of Buddhist ethics to the contemporary social scenario in which modern man is placed. The Buddhist ideals come to the rescue of humankind only when they are understood and practised in their right spirit. Thus the present work looks at Buddhist ethics both from normative and applied perspectives.

We would also like to express our indebtedness to Dr Kona Radhakrishna Murty, Reader in Philosophy, C.S.R. Sarma College, Ongole. He received his training in Buddhist Studies from the well-known Pāli scholar in India, Professor Mahesh Tiwari of University of Delhi. His study on Buddhist Values provided valuable insights.

M.V. Ram Kumar Ratnam
K. Srinivas

Contents

Introduction

EVERY philosophy sets forth certain ideals to be emulated. Sometimes the ideals set forth by a particular philosophy remain utopian for they can neither be experientially realised nor be successfully translated into concrete realities. Contrary to an utopian ideal, a genuine ideal is that which can be realised and practised by individuals in their day-to-day life. Such ideal has its own meaning and purpose. Mere reification of ideals, which are of no practical consequences in one's life in particular and society in general, amounts to nurturing philosophical idealism of a dogmatic kind. The genuineness of any philosophical system lies in its ability to contribute, directly or indirectly, to the life-world shared by everyone of us in the realisation of the purpose and meaning of life. The grand philosophical traditions of the Orient and the Occident shared such a view.

It is traditionally believed that philosophy as a reflective enterprise is not only concerned with the essential meaning and purpose of life but also with human activities. In other words, philosophy ought to be the philosophy of life. It cannot be separated from the day-to-day existential problems of the individuals. As a matter of fact, the philosophy of any people represents their feelings, thinking, and living. Thus philosophy is anthropocentric. The philosophy of Buddhism is one such philosophy that does not segregate theory and practice. The teachings of the Buddha are true ideals for they can be realised by every individual in his/her own life. They are far from being utopian. The success of the Buddhist philosophy as a progressive one lies in its ability to transform the lives of millions of people all over the globe. It advocated whatever is conducive for good and healthy human life and society. As observed by one of the well-known contemporary French philosophers, Emmanuel Levinas (1906-95), a sound philosophical system could be erected not on metaphysical or epistemological foundations but only on firm ethical foundations. This is what we could see in the Buddhist philosophy. The philosophy of Buddhism is primarily a philosophy intended to put forth a form of ethics that is aimed at self-perfection. But in the process, the self-regarding virtues gradually take shape as other-regarding virtues. In fact, one can see the amalgamation of philosophical, religious and moral ideals in the fundamental doctrines of Buddhism. Of course, the interdependence of philosophical, religious and moral ideals is one of the chief traits of the Oriental philosophies.

According to Aristotle, the essential feature of human beings is rationality. Therefore, humans are not only inquisitive but also capable of self-introspection. Also, it is this essential feature (rationality) that demarcates human beings from other living creatures. But human rationality is two-pronged in the sense that it has two important dimensions, namely, scientific and moral. The rapid developments in the realm of science and technology clearly establish the view that scientific rationality has reached its pinnacle. The material growth of any society is invariably linked up with the developments in science and technology. But science cannot be the paradigm of human life. The decadent forms of morality witnessed in the industrialised or soft totalitarian (consumerist) societies justify our belief that our moral rationality has reached its nadir. In such societies human suffering is conspicuous, for the affluent alone enjoy sensuous pleasures at the cost of those who are economically weak and deprived. There is no space left for love and compassion in such societies. A section of human beings is treated as a means by the economically and politically powerful section of society to achieve their ends. But they hardly realise that the sensuous pleasures are not the *summum bonum* of human life. One who is accustomed to lead a life of sensuous pleasures looks for more and more material wealth for otherwise he cannot lead such a life. The desire to amass more and more material wealth breeds greed in a person. And greed takes away one's peace. Lack of peace in one's life is also a form of suffering. Therefore, it is a misconception to think that affluent are spared from suffering. If it were so, the kings and queens must be the happiest persons on the Earth, but the history of humankind reveals that they too were not spared by suffering. Sickness and old age rain on the rich and poor alike. A well-balanced society is that which gives importance to both scientific and moral forms of rationality. Scientific realism sans moral idealism reduces human individual to the level of a beast. Similarly, moral idealism sans scientific realism reduces human individual to the level of a stoic and an ascetic. The philosophy of Buddhism does not subscribe to any of these two extremes. Like Aristotle's principle of "golden mean," the philosophy of Buddhism advocates the "middle path." It is not an exaggeration to say that a true religion is the religion of humanity in which one does not find any distinction between religion and philosophy. They are fused into one. The religious philosophies of the Orient are the best examples for such a fusion.

However, the anthropocentric purport of any religious-philosophical tradition does not rule out humans' concern for other living creatures on the Earth. Man is part and parcel of the natural world. In this natural world he creates a social world for the benefit and the furtherance of the human race. As aptly stated by Aristotle, God and beasts do not require a society for "man is naturally a political animal and that one who is not a citizen of any state, if the cause of his isolation be natural and not accidental, is either a superhuman being or low in the scale of civilisation, as he stands alone like a "blot" on the backgammon board."[1] Since God or the Supreme Power is one and only one, we, as ordinary individuals, cannot attain the status of God to escape from our social commitments. However, one can escape from one's social commitments by being indifferent to society and to fellow individuals living in society. In other words, one can choose to lead a life of beast. To lead beastly life one does require neither religion nor philosophy nor science. But to qualify oneself as a human being one needs to be a member of society in which one finds a diversity of human relationships. The bedrock of all human relationships existing in a society is what we call culture in general. The culture of any society is reflected in the lifestyle led by the members of that society. Although Buddhism does not subscribe to the existence of any supreme God or godhead its concern for society (*saṁgha*) is something remarkable. It is the *saṁgha* that reminds every individual of his/her duties as obligations towards other individuals and living creatures. Of course, no one denies the contribution made by science and technology to the modern world in various spheres of human life. Science provides us with all earthly pleasures, which are non-enduring. It may provide us with temporal comforts. To weigh or judge every aspect of life in terms of science leads to scientism. Such a view turns science into an ideology. According to Marx, an ideology is a false consciousness that deprives individuals of free thinking. As we know anything in excess leads to disasters. It has to be properly balanced. The consequences of modern science are known to everyone. People have become more and more materialistic and there is no end for greed. The unwarranted competition in every

1. Aristotle, *The Politics*, Book I, ch. 2, trans., J.E.C. Welldon, London, 1885.

sphere of life has led to wars and violence of different types. All these are manifestations of suffering. To alleviate human suffering moral rationality of the individuals has to be strengthened. In the absence of moral rationality the life of human beings is going to be much worse. Long ago the Buddha recognised this fact. He could see suffering all over.

The sole remedy to the maladies of the modern world lies in the recognition of human values, and care for human life. If one realises that human birth is precious, its continuance is also very important. The fundamental ethical precepts of Buddhism remind us of this fact. The reason why the ethics of Buddhism appeals to one who loves and cares for human life is that it makes one realise the existential situation in which one is placed. In the absence of morality an individual is not different from a beast. In other words, as rightly observed by Plato, his rational part is dominated by his irrational part that consists of appetite and spirit. Although the goal of Buddhism is to attain *nibbāna/nirvāṇa*, its practical approach to various problems of life is something worthy of emulation. For instance, non-injury, non-stealing, benevolence, charity, and liberality are the virtues to be emulated by every individual. The Four Noble Truths (*āriya sacca/ārya satya*) of the Buddha are worth knowing and their philosophical implications have to be realised by one and all.

The Buddha was primarily an ethical teacher rather than a philosopher. He never entertained speculative questions posed to him by his own disciples for they are of no use in tackling the problems of day-to-day life. What really concerned the Buddha was an immediate release of individuals from suffering. His method is simple and practical. He used to enlighten his disciples with simple stories. He never used any complicated methods or philosophical techniques to make them realise the meaning and purpose of life. This is clearly seen from the ethical precepts advanced by him. People like Mahatma Gandhi, Ambedkar and many great social reformers in India and elsewhere in the world came under the influence of the Buddhist ideals. They made use of the fundamental ethical teachings of Buddhism to emancipate people from social problems of their time. The survival and the continued influence of the Buddhist ethics for centuries together speak about its elasticity. It is not a rigid and rigorous moral exercise to be practised by an individual in one's private life by abandoning one's social responsibilities. In fact, the relevance of the Buddhist ethics to the contemporary social world makes it more profound and desirable. The peculiar kinds of social problems confronted by us are of horrifying type. They are the result of the dominating power of modern science and technology. The technological consciousness has thrown our moral values overboard. There is a drastic change in the lifestyle of the individuals. There is no belief in the view that science is value neutral and is the embodiment of human dignity. The reason is that we have become slaves to our passions. The source of these passions is not within us but from without. The domination of science and technology is the real source of these passions. We completely lost control over science and technology. Instead science and technology started controlling our lives. The natural consequence of such domination is our failure to distinguish good from evil, eternal from non-eternal, genuine values from artificial ones, happiness from pleasures, emotions from passions, genuine needs from false ones. We are only living in an artificial paradise. The trivialisation of human values in the contemporary society has led to violation of human rights, war and violence, suicide and euthanasia, abortion and contraception, gender inequality, and homo-sexuality and so on. Desire (*moha*), lack of contentment, and perversions of mind are chiefly responsible for these social evils. Modern science acts as a catalyst for these social evils. Test-tube babies, cloning, gene transplantation, change of sex are the creations of modern science. Science as such is not to be blamed for this state of affairs. It is the scientists behind these discoveries or inventions who are to be blamed. A scientist must realise that he is first a human being then only a scientist. Electricity does not spare anyone including one who discovered it from shock when anyone comes into direct contact with it. Similar is the case with science. If science is harmful, it is harmful to entire humanity including the scientists who are instrumental in designing such dreadful devices. The belief that a doctor never suffers from any disease is a myth. Therefore, one must beware of excessive dose of science at the cost of morality.

It is a known fact that children are the building blocks of future societies. The need of the hour is that they must be inculcated with the Buddhist ideals such as non-violence, tolerance, non-falsehood, non-stealing, sympathy, love kindness, charity, reverence for elders and teachers, gratitude and so on. These ideals can be part of any value education. Similarly, drinking, smoking, overeating, wearing gaudy and rich ornaments or dress must be restricted. If children are trained in practising these virtues then the society in which they live would be benefited a lot. Greed, contempt, and jealousy are the vices to be despised. Children must be told to deride such vices.

Although there is no special method employed in analysing the ethical precepts of Buddhism in the present work, there is an attempt to highlight the significance of Buddhist ethics and its relevance to contemporary society. The Buddhist ethics is not restricted to any caste, creed, race, religion, region, and language. Like Kant's "categorical imperative," Buddhist ethics has universal application. It is left to us to make use of it in a wholesome manner for the well-being of individuals as well as society. The ethical precepts of Buddhism are laid down in accordance with the habits or moral ideas of those days. These precepts can be amended to cater to the needs of modern society. Thus an amount of flexibility is inbuilt in the ethical doctrines of Buddhism. For instance, violence of any sort is not welcomed by Buddhism. But in the case of unprovoked violence, there is nothing wrong in going for self-defence. This cannot be treated as violence. The ethical instructions of Buddhism always do not have negative form. There are several moral instructions which are positive and are applicable not to monks and nuns alone but to every human being worthy of leading good life. For instance, the instruction that to keep away from a fool and get associated with wise alone has a positive role to play in one's life. Likewise, one must be well-trained in any art of one's choice so that he is honoured by every one. To speak pleasant words, and to be respectful to elders are not meant for any particular community or caste, religious followers, creed or race and so on. One must train one's mind to be unshaken in contact with the conditions of the world, free from sorrow and defilement.

Buddhist ethics is both autonomous and heteronomous in its character. It is autonomous in so far as its teachings are aimed at individual self-perfection and heteronomous when they are aimed at the perfection of entire society. It is hard to imagine a person is moral in isolation from society. None can think of a moral code of his own a priori. It is also absolutely impossible for a person to be a mute spectator to the external moral influences that constantly work on him. His ethical code is an outcome of the admixture of maxims, traditions, customs, practices, and prevailing ideas in the society in which he is an organic part. Apart from this fact, any community, school or sect which is founded on common religious beliefs or ethical principles would naturally require a particular religious training or moral education. This is the case with Buddhism too. No one would deny such an education for moulding them, so to speak, into the "Buddhist type." The ethical precepts advocated by Buddhism, though subtle in some respects, are nothing but general guidance to show the direction in which the Buddhist ought to turn on his way to final salvation.

The practical character of the Buddhist ethics is conspicuous. The Buddha was more concerned with existential problems faced by the individuals in their day-to-day life. The ethical precepts of Buddhism are basically taken from *Tipiṭakas*, namely, *Sutta-Piṭaka, Vinaya-Piṭaka*, and *Abhidhamma-Piṭaka*. The *Sutta-Piṭaka* contains within itself *Dīgha-Nikāya*, a collection of 34 long treatises; *Majjhima-Nikāya*, a collection of 152 treatises; *Saṁyutta-Nikāya*; *Aṅguttara-Nikāya*; and *Khuddaka-Nikāya*. The *Vinaya-Piṭaka* consists of *Sutta Vibhaṅga*; the *Khandhas*; and the *Parivarsapatha*. The *Abhidhamma-Piṭaka* consists of *Dhamma, Vibhaṅga, Kathāvatthu, Puggala, Dhātu, Jamaka*, and *Paṭṭhāna*. Of course, there is ample evidence to show that the sacred books of Buddhism over a period of time have undergone many changes in the form of additions and alterations. But these additions and alterations are made without losing sight of the fundamental ethical tenets of Buddhism.

The present work is classified into six chapters apart from introduction. The first chapter deals with an overview of Buddhism as a philosophical doctrine with a view to highlighting the philosophical and ethical foundations of Buddhism. This account helps us as a necessary backdrop in analysing the cardinal ethical doctrines of Buddhism. The ethics of Buddhism is invariably linked up with the Buddhist theory of causation that is explained in terms of the Doctrine of Dependent Origination (*paticca-samuppāda/pratītya-samutpāda*). In addition to that a brief account of the Four Noble Truths (*āriya saccāni/ārya satya*) is also given, for they represent the quintessence of the philosophy of Buddhism.

The second chapter on the classification of Buddhist ethics

brings out the classification of the fundamental ethical precepts of Buddhism into five, eight and ten in order to show their relevance to monks, nuns, laymen, and non-Buddhists. This classification is absolutely necessary as it traces back the practices of Buddhism since time immemorial, and subsequently the changes incorporated in the fundamental doctrines of Buddhism with a view to showing their relevance to the present social circumstances.

The third chapter aims at showing the autonomous character of Buddhist ethics. In this chapter an attempt has been made to show that the ethical precepts of Buddhism have to be followed by an individual on his own without depending on their effects on others for self-perfection. However, it also tries to establish that self-regarding activities of an individual ultimately lead to the other-regarding activities. In a sense Buddhist ethics is a mixture of both autonomous and heteronomous characteristics.

The fourth chapter is an attempt to highlight the ethical idealism of Buddhism with a view to showing that the fundamental ethical doctrines of Buddhism are not idealistic in the sense that they are not utopian, but dystopian in their character, and the ideals of Buddhist ethics are highly practicable and can be translated into concrete realities. Therefore, they are not ideals of reification, but ideals with a pragmatic purport.

The fifth chapter deals with the contemporary social evils like violation of human rights, war, suicide and euthanasia, abortion and contraception, gender inequality, and homosexuality and the Buddhist solution to these problems. Each issue has been dealt with elaborately to see how far the ethical doctrines of Buddhism would come to our rescue in solving these social problems faced by the individuals in the various parts of the globe.

While concluding the present work the general reflections on the subject matter are presented with a view to showing that Buddhist ethics has its relevance to contemporary social life in spite of the fact that its sole aim is to get oneself emancipated from this world. At the same time Buddhism does not neglect the problems faced by human individuals in their existential situation.

At the end select bibliography is provided for the benefit of the readers for further advanced research in this field.

1

Fundamental Tenets of Buddhism

Background

GOTAMA Siddattha/Gautama Siddhārtha, who is popularly known as the Buddha, was born in 563 BCE into the royal Sākya/Śākya clan of Kapilavatthu/Kapilavastu in Lumbinī situated on the lower slopes of the Himalayas. His mother Mahāmāyā died when Gautama was barely seven days old and he was brought up by his father Śuddhodana by extending all possible comforts to the young Prince. The teachings of the Buddha evoked the admiration not only from his followers but also from the orthodox Indians for their clarity and simplicity. The gentle and noble character of the Buddha made him a role model for humanity. His teachings gained popularity as a way of life (Buddhism) for their progressive outlook and pragmatic approach. Buddhism is not a religion in the sense in which the Westerners treat it, for the Buddha never claimed that he was the God-incarnate. It is only the followers of the teachings of the Buddha who deservedly elevated him to the status of God; and the teachings of the Buddha are given the status of a Gospel for they are worthy of emulation. Unlike Western religions, which are by and large God-centric, the religions of the Orient are concerned with ultimate human destiny or liberation. Thus they have soteriological purport. In this sense Buddhism is both a religion and a philosophy. The Buddha was a great social reformer and a prophet of love, compassion, and non-violence. As a dialectician, the Buddha established the law of eternal change as the base and core of his philosophy. The Buddhist philosophy arose as an ideological reaction to the then existing Brāhmanism or the Upaniṣadic philosophy, which was highly metaphysical and ritualistic. The Upaniṣads tried to discover some unchanging, eternal reality behind all changing and temporary phenomena of the empirical world. This quest for the absolute led them to the concept of Self (*Atta/Ātman*) and the notion of *Brahman*, the Supreme Reality. Consequently, the intellectuals of that time concentrated more on renunciation and penance, and on the methods of realising the Self (*Atta/Ātman*). The questions — Is this world eternal or not? Is there life after death or not? Is the Self or Soul independent of the material body or not? — were treated as the most fundamental questions of philosophy. The great sages and seers engaged themselves in unending and hair-splitting controversies about these problems. The Buddha himself spent some time in finding answers to these questions, but ultimately found them to be nonsensical and useless for the life of existence. He naturally turned his attention to the existential problems rather than addressing any metaphysical questions, for they do not lead to any meaningful end. What caused the drastic change in the Buddha's attitude towards human life is the sight of suffering and death undergone by humankind.[1]

It is a gross misconception on the part of those scholars who believe that Buddhism is driven out of the Indian soil just because of its anti-Brāhmanical stand. To quote the remarks of one of the well-acclaimed contemporary Indian philosophers, P.T. Raju, in this context:

> One will be justified also in saying that it has not disappeared from India, but forms part of the life-blood of Indian outlook

1. R. Puligandla, *Fundamentals of Indian Philosophy*, New Delhi: D.K. Printworld (P) Ltd., 1997, p. 33.

> and culture; for the Buddha is still venerated as an incarnation of the supreme God-head in its aspects as mercy and compassion (*karuṇā*), and his philosophical and ethico-religious concepts are incorporated into all the great philosophies of spiritual life.[2]

The great social reformers of the Indian subcontinent, including Mahatma Gandhi, were influenced by the Buddhist ideals. The concept of *ahiṁsā* is the Buddha's gift to humankind. Just as Platonism is not dead in the Western culture and outlook, Buddhism is also not dead in the Indian culture and outlook. The Buddha never put his teachings in a written form. Therefore, it was a daunting task to the followers of the Buddha to fix his teachings. Four important councils were held to fix the teachings of the Buddha in Rājagṛha (483 BCE), Vaiśālī (383 BCE), Pāṭaliputra (249 BCE), and Peshawar or Julandhar or some place in Kashmir (CE 100), according to the historians. And it is believed that the more than 60 per cent of the Buddhist Canon was compiled during the first council itself. The Canon includes the famous three baskets of Buddhism. What is important to notice is that all the sects of Buddhism accept the Canonical literature although their practices may differ from one sect to another.

The Pāli Canon

The literature available on Buddhism is very vast and rich. It is customary to classify it into: Hīnayāna and Mahāyāna. The former is written in Pāli and the latter in Sanskrit. The kernel of Hīnayāna literature is known as Pāli Canon. It is also known as *Tipiṭaka/Tripiṭaka* meaning three baskets. Like other great ancient teachers, the Buddha taught orally. But his teachings were in the form of sermons or dialogues. The Pāli Canon was composed long after the demise of the Buddha. It is

2. P.T. Raju, *Structural Depths of Indian Thought*, New Delhi: South Asia Publishers, 1985, p. 146.

generally regarded as the authentic teaching of the Buddha as revealed by his closest disciples and confidants. The first basket is called *Vinaya-Piṭaka,* which contains the rules of conduct and the discipline of the order, the Saṁgha; the second is the *Sutta-Piṭaka* (also known as the Nikāyas), a collection of the sayings, sermons, and the dialogues of the Buddha; and the third basket, the *Abhidhamma-Piṭaka,* is a discussion on the matters pertinent to philosophy. The non-Canonical part of Hīnayāna literature includes such works as the *Milindapañha,* the *Visuddhimagga,* the *Dīpavaṁsa,* the *Mahāvaṁsa,* and innumerable commentaries on the *Tipiṭaka/ Tripiṭaka.* The Mahāyāna literature is even vaster and more prolific. During the long period of development and the spread of Buddhism outside the boundaries of the Indian subcontinent, most of the Mahāyāna works were translated from Sanskrit into Tibetan and Chinese. Unfortunately, a good number of Sanskrit texts left in India are lost.

Noble Character

The Buddha was an original thinker besides being a moral prophet. He was wholeheartedly inclined to liberate humanity from suffering. The qualities of being a thinker and a prophet made him noble and humble in his pronouncements. The Buddha's analysis of the problem of suffering and his overall emphasis on the practical aspects of morality and conduct leading to the conquest of suffering reveal that he was more interested in tackling the immediate existential problems of humankind rather than dealing with matters pertinent to the other-world. Not only that, the Buddha was primarily a moral philosopher but not a metaphysician. The most urgent and important task for him is to alleviate the suffering of humankind. This led him to earn the name "the great physician." When a person is struck by a poisonous arrow and is wriggling with pain, the first and foremost thing to offer him is to remove the arrow out of the wounded part of his body in order to mitigate the pain. At this stage it is useless to elicit the information as to how this arrow struck him, the man who shot this arrow and so on. Thus the approach of the Buddha was more pragmatic. The Buddha not only exhibited humility, but also pointed out that whatever he taught must not be reduced to a dogma by his disciples.

Critique of Scholasticism

In the first place, Buddhism launched a frontal attack on scholasticism, which encouraged dogmatism and completely discouraged free thinking. Scholasticism was rooted in some absolute and rigid categories. The Buddha in his very first discourse at Varanasi (Banāras) held that:[3]

> Let us put aside such unprofitable and unsolvable questions (*avyaktāni*) as the questions of beginning and end. I will teach you *dhamma*. That being thus this comes to be. From the coming to be of that, this arises. That being absent, this does not happen. From the cessation of that this ceases. This is the *dhamma*. Whoever accepts *dhamma*, accepts the law of *paticca-samuppāda* (dependent origination).

The Doctrine of Dependent Origination (*paticca-samuppāda/ pratītya-samutpāda*) is the core of the Buddhist philosophy. Nothing exists by itself, for nothing is absolute. Everything depends on something else. Everything is the effect of some cause. As long as the cause exists the effect also persists. When the cause ceases to be, the effect also vanishes. Everything is relative. Cause and effect are interrelated. One thing flows from the other. The Buddha developed this principle further in his later discourses and with the help of his philosophy of change he shattered the concepts of eternal Self (*Atta/Ātman*)

---

3. Y. Balaramamoorty, "Buddhist Philosophy" in Rahul Sankrityayan and others (eds.), *Buddhism: The Marxist Approach*, New Delhi: People's Publishing House, 1978, p. 39.

and *Brahman*. Although the Buddha advised people not to bother about the scholastic questions of beginning and end, he actually answered those questions through his Doctrine of Dependent Origination. Thus the most fundamental tenet of Buddhism is non-eternality. In fact, this expression has been gradually replaced by the word "momentary." In other words, Buddhism holds that whatever is real is "momentary" or "dynamic" and whatever is not momentary is not real. Thus the Buddhist philosophy of change is akin to the "flux" philosophy of Heraclitus. As a matter of fact, the Buddhist denial of God or soul is a natural corollary of this principle. The *anatta-vāda/anātma-vāda* of Buddhism has its own importance.

The dynamic character of the Buddhist philosophy has completely transformed the very art of philosophising about the world and man's place in it. Even those who believe in the eternality of reality or the self have admitted the fact that there is something called external world, and is ever changing. However, they held that there is an eternal principle in this world of change. This they called *Brahman / Ātman*. Analogically, the Buddhists explain their position by narrating the following example. When we look into the trunk of a banana tree we would only find layers after layers, but no substance within it. Similarly, the things in the world do not contain eternal substance, namely, *Brahman / Ātman*. The empirical world or the world of experience is devoid of any eternal element. Hence the notion of *sunnatā / śūnyatā* or void explains the Buddhist notion of dynamism as against the Upaniṣadic conception of permanence. The Buddhists hold that the clouds go on changing each moment; so does this world. The changes being imperceptible we do not easily encounter them in our sensory experience. Even the most solid diamond or iron goes on changing every moment, however imperceptible these changes may be. Then why should anyone attribute similarity or sameness in their previous or subsequent forms? According to Buddhism, similarity is organisation. The effect is always similar to its cause; hence there is always an illusion of sameness. The flame of the lamp is changing every moment but the new flame born out of the old flame is similar to it. This makes us conclude that it is the same flame.

Theory of Causation

The notion of impermanence or change is linked up with the Doctrine of Dependent Origination (*paticca-samuppāda/pratītya-samutpāda*). In this scheme of things it is held that cause and effect are interlinked. But how long does the cause exist? It is not eternal. If it is not eternal, then it cannot produce an effect that is eternal. Therefore, the effect is something momentary. The effect itself transforms into a cause to produce another effect. The process goes on like this. The integration and disintegration of things lead to the origination and destruction of things of the empirical world. Since there are no immutable or eternal first principles, there are no things (objects) in the world but only events (*dhamma/dharma*). This view of Buddhism is akin to the view of earlier Wittgenstein expressed in his *Tractatus Logico-Philosophicus*. According to him, the world does not consist of things or objects, but only of facts. The facts of Wittgenstein are nothing but the events (*dhamma/dharma*) of Buddhism. The events come into existence and vanish. They have mere temporal existence.

Buddhists further explained the law of causation in the following manner. To put it in the language of the Buddha: "When this was, then this comes and it was then this becomes (*asmin sati idam bhavati*)."[4] At the completion of this, this is born. What has just ended is the cause and what has emerged after the cause is the effect. The effect was wholly non-existent

4. Rahul Sankrityayan, "Buddhist Dialectics" in Rahul Sankrityayan et al. (eds.), *Buddhism: The Marxist Approach*, p. 5.

when the cause was there, and when the effect came into existence the cause completely vanished. There was no eternal substance to be transferred to the effect. Actually they have no other relation to each other except that the one preceded or followed the other. Similar view is advanced by the British empiricist David Hume in his analysis of causation. According to Hume, there is no necessary connection between cause and effect. In a way, it is one event giving the way for the other. The antecedent is called cause and the consequence effect. Such an association between one event and another is formed on the basis of habit and custom.

The Doctrine of Dependent Origination becomes inevitable to explain the nature of the world when it is seen as a conglomerate of events, which are under constant flux. The dynamic nature of reality and the strong conviction that there is no eternal substratum forced the Buddhists to subscribe to the view that the world is made up of events. Likewise, the rejection of the traditional view of causation invariably led to the Doctrine of Dependent Origination. This doctrine of Buddhists virtually shattered another old myth, according to which a cause produces one or more effects. The Upaniṣadic sages believed in several strange phenomena originating from the same Self (*Atta*/*Ātman*). Even in our day-to-day world one element is called the cause and the other originating from it the effect. The Buddhist philosophy contended that no event, or to use their nomenclature *dhamma*, is born of one thing. An effect will not spring from one cause but from multiplicity of causes. This theory is called collectivity of causes (*hetu-samaggivāda/hetu-samagrivāda*).

The great Buddhist philosopher Dharmakīrti held that: "One (thing) is not born out of one but all is born of collective causes."[5] The effect is produced out of the multiplicity of

5. Rahul Sankrityayan et al. (eds.), *Buddhism: The Marxist Approach*, p. 6.

causes. Although the doctrine of unity of opposites is not mentioned here, yet it is presumed that one effect is the result of the coming together of the multiplicity of causes. If any one of them is missing from the unity then the supposed effect would not come into existence. Also, it is important to notice, according to Buddhism, that cause is entirely different from the effect. In other words, the emergence of the effect is a qualitative change. This theory is popularly known as *asatkārya-vāda,* according to which the effect does not pre-exist in the cause. It is something totally new. And this qualitative change cannot take place unless all the causes are pooled in the required measure or quantity. The Buddhist theory of causation suggests that there is always something new emerging out of the old. Thus history is not a mere repetition of the old events. Human civilisation is a gradual progression from the lower to the higher and further on. As held by Hegel, it is the gradual unfolding of reason. The philosophy of Buddhism believes in the human progress. The law of change is an inevitable one.

The Notion of Real

In the light of the above-mentioned analysis of the empirical world, Buddhism had to define anew what is "real (*sat*)" and what is "unreal (*asat*)." The ancient Upaniṣadic philosophers did not find it difficult to distinguish real from unreal. They held that what is eternal is real and what is temporal is unreal. In the philosophy of Buddhism, there is no room for such real(s), for there is nothing eternal. The "real," according to the Buddhists, is that which is capable of producing objective and pragmatic result (*artha-kriyā-sāmarthyam*). We treat food, water, and shelter as real for they are capable of fulfilling the basic existential needs of all living creatures. Thus they have both objective and pragmatic purport. Anything that satisfies objective and pragmatic purport within a given existential situation is not just real, but absolutely real. For the Buddhists, a thing need not be eternal in order to be real. What was "real" for the ancient Upaniṣadic seers and sages is incapable of objective and pragmatic purport, for it is immutable, eternal, and static. What is the proof of existence of an inactive thing that is beyond the reach of the senses? It is neither an object of direct perception nor of inference based on it. The criterion of being objectively active is an infallible test of reality. The real should prove itself by its objective participation. What is real cannot be established on the basis of mere reason. The rationalists may disagree with this view. In fact, Kant in his *Critique of Pure Reason* tried to show the limitations of pure reason. According to him, reason only aids sense perception to conceptualise our perceptual experience. Kant's remark that concepts (categories of understanding) without percepts (sensible intuitions) are empty; and percepts without concepts are blind may appeal to a genuine Buddhist. Hegel, the German absolute idealist, in his *Phenomenology of Spirit* went to the extent of saying that "all real is rational and all rational is real." Such a view is unacceptable to phenomenalists and also to realists. According to Dharmakīrti, reason is not the final authority. He held that: "if the objects themselves are like that, who are we?"[6] If the nature of objects is known through mere rational powers, then the human nature is not an exception to this rule. It is ridiculous and non-illuminating to say that reason is the sole source of our knowledge of reality. This does not in any way mean that the Buddhists are irrational. Their intention is not to run down the reason, but only to show its limitations. If the Buddhists are irrational just because they oppose the dominance of reason as the only legitimate source of knowledge, then the same rule is equally applicable to Kant also. But none would accept that the Buddhists and Kant are irrational. Their rationality is depicted

6. Rahul Sankrityayan et al. (eds.), *Buddhism: The Marxist Approach*, p. 7.

in the way in which they treated the role of reason in comprehending the nature of reality. They only objected to the primacy of reason over sense-experience, but did not deny the role of reason in our day-to-day affairs. It is the objective and pragmatic purport that is the benchmark or touchstone of reality. All our day-to-day dealings are rooted in this principle of objectivity.

The Four Noble Truths (Ariya Saccani/Ārya Satya)

Life, according to Buddhism, is full of suffering (*dukkha/ duḥkha*). In other words, life is identical with suffering. To live is to suffer in one way or another. This is not an exaggeration, but a truism. If we examine the phenomenon of life we notice one thing in abundance; that is suffering. This all-pervading fact of suffering has become the central issue for the philosophy of Buddhism. Want, hunger, greed, jealousy, anxiety, animosity, egoism, sickness, old age, and death are too apparent for us that we cannot fail to notice them. Frustration, disappointment for not being able to achieve or obtain what is desired, and the pain at the thought of losing anything dearer to us are also various manifestations of suffering. Of course, the critiques of Buddhism held that it is wrong on the part of the Buddha to conclude that human life is full of suffering, for the suffering is noticed only in contrast to something that does not amount to suffering (pleasure). Both pleasure and pain are evenly balanced. If it were the case what made the Buddha to project only on the darker side of human life? The answer to this objection is that what appears to be pleasure at the moment eventually ceases to be pleasure by leading to boredom or dissatisfaction. It is only due to the myopic vision people think that there is pleasure in opposition to pain. What they fail to notice is that every pleasure contains within itself the elements or seeds of pain that surface at one time or another. The peak of all suffering is death, which destroys all our hopes and aspirations. Everyone has to experience death. As rightly remarked by Martin Heidegger, there is no death by proxy. Similarly, Wittgenstein viewed that death is not an event in one's own life. The very thought of death itself may cause or produce the fear or anxiety in us, which is a form of suffering. This is the case with every human being. Therefore, asked the Buddha — How can anyone be blind to this glaring fact, namely, universal suffering?

The expression *dukkha/duḥkha* is often regarded as suffering in the sense of physical and psychological pain. But, the philosophy of Buddhism has provided us with a radical understanding of the notion of suffering by equating it with impermanence (*anitta/anitya*).[7] Impermanence is the basic characteristic of all existence. It includes both animate and inanimate facts of life. When we see around we find constant change in the objects of the world. There appears to be nothing consistent or permanent. The philosophy of Buddhism highlights the fact that it is this impermanence that is the root cause of suffering. If people do not lose what they have, and obtain what they do not have, if they do not perish or die, then there is no suffering. But this is not the case with our day-to-day life. An incisive analysis of our day-to-day existence clearly shows that everything is constantly changing. Therefore, an unchanging and permanent world alone can be the source of happiness. But, it is nothing but a figment of imagination and the product of wishful thinking. The fundamental characteristic of reality, emphasised the Buddha, which we experience is impermanence. Thus the First Noble Truth is that existence *per se* is impermanence (*dukkha/duḥkha*).

The Second Noble Truth is that suffering is the result of certain conditions that constitute the very essence of existence.

---

7. Walpola Rahula, *What the Buddha Taught*, New York: Grove Press, 1962, pp. 17-20.

Accordingly, suffering is not a product of mere chance but brought about by certain conditions that constitute the very core of existence. If suffering is uncaused, then there can be no way of eradicating or eliminating it. It is worth mentioning here that every phenomenon, including our sensations, feelings, desires, impulses, sickness, old age and death, is produced by the causes that themselves are phenomena. In other words, the entire existence, as we experience it, is a vast causal nexus. This fact is expressed by the formula: "This arising, that arises; this ceasing to be, that ceases to be," or equivalently, "This phenomenon is dependent upon that phenomenon."[8] It amounts to saying that nothing exists unconditionally and absolutely. Everything is dependent on something other than itself. The doctrine that everything is caused is known as the Doctrine of Dependent Origination (*paticca-samuppāda/pratītya-samutpāda*). It is the fundamental principle of the teachings of the Buddha. All the schools of Buddhism unequivocally accept this view. Thus the Second Noble Truth may be summarised in the following manner. Suffering (*dukkha/duḥkha*), like anything else, is dependent upon certain conditions. It amounts to saying that suffering has a cause. The various conditions that are responsible for the production of suffering are explained by the Buddha in the form of a chain of causes and effects made up of 12 links. Hence "the twelvefold theory of causation" is another name for the Doctrine of Dependent Origination. The links are as follows. We first observe that if an individual is not at all born, then the question of his experiencing suffering does not arise at all. But an individual cannot be born unless there is will to be born. The will to be born is due to individual's clinging to objects — physical and mental. But what is the source of craving? It arises out of our sense-experience. If we did not have sense-experience, then there would be no objects

---

8. *Mahā-Nidāna-Sutta of the Dīgha-Nikāya* (trs.), pp. 202-8.

for us to crave. How is sense-experience possible? Sense-experience arises out of the contact between senses and objects. In the absence of this contact between senses and objects there would not be any sense-experience. How do sense-object contacts arise? The contacts are the result of the six sense organs of cognition, including the mind. These sense organs in turn are dependent upon the embryonic psycho-physical organism. But the embryonic organism itself depends upon some initial consciousness. What makes this initial consciousness possible? The initial consciousness arises out of impressions (kārmic forces) from past experience. Finally, these kārmic forces themselves are the result of ignorance. Where there can be no ignorance, there can be no kārmic forces and impressions. The following are the twelve links:

1. Ignorance (*avijjā/avidyā*)
2. Kārmic impressions (*saṅkhāra/saṁsāra*)
3. Initial embryonic consciousness (*vinnāna/vijñāna*)
4. Embryonic psycho-physical organism (*nāma-rūpa*)
5. Six sense organs, including mind (*ṣadāyatana*)
6. Sense-object contact (*sparśa*)
7. Sense-experience (*vedanā*)
8. Thirst for sense-objects (*tṛṣṇā*)
9. Clinging (*upādāna*)
10. Will to be born (*bhava*)
11. Birth or rebirth (*jāti*)
12. Suffering, sickness, old age, and death (*jamma-maraṇa/ jarā-maraṇa*)

In the above list, the first two factors pertain to past life, factors third to ten to present life, and the last two to future life. It is also to be noted that the twelvefold chain is not a linear one but a circular chain.[9] The twelfth factor is again linked to the first. What is to be noticed in this chain is that some of the links are only necessary conditions but not sufficient conditions for the ones that follow them. Thus old age and death are only necessary but not sufficient conditions of ignorance. Likewise, sense-experience is only a necessary condition but not a sufficient one for thirst and desire. The links in the chain are mere necessary conditions but none of them by itself is a sufficient condition. If all necessary conditions are reduced to sufficient condition, then the old age and death would necessarily bring about ignorance. And since humans do become old and die they would forever be caught up in ignorance and go through the cycles of birth and death without ever being able to break the chain and get out of the cycle of causation. Not only that, the chain has no beginning in time. In other words, it did not begin at some moment in time. This is another way of saying that ignorance has no beginning. However, by following the Buddhist path one can break the chain in order to attain liberation (*nibbāna/ nirvāṇa*) by eradicating ignorance, which is the root cause of all suffering. Unlike in the Western tradition, in Buddhism the primordial burden of an individual is not original sin but original ignorance. Ignorance is identified with suffering and bondage. It can only be overcome by means of knowledge and wisdom (*paññā/prajñā*).

The twelve links of causation, which is the foundation of all the other teachings of the Buddha, is variously referred to as the *dhamma-cakra/dharma-cakra* or the Wheel of Becoming, *saṅkhāra-cakra/saṁsāra-cakra* or the Wheel of Existence, *jamma-maraṇa-cakra/janma-maraṇa-cakra* or the Wheel of Birth and Death, *bhāva-cakra* or the Wheel of Rebirth, *dvādaśa-nidāna* or the Twelve Sources, and *paticca-samuppāda/pratītya-samutpāda* or Dependent Origination.

9. *Mahā-Vagga* (trs.), p. 840.

Once we come to know the causes of suffering, now the question before us is how to eradicate them. This leads us to the Third Noble Truth of the philosophy of Buddhism. Since suffering is caused, it can be eradicated by eliminating its cause. The cessation of suffering can be brought about by removal of the conditions on which suffering is dependent. Once we remove these causes of suffering, then we become free from all the fetters of existence. Then, what is that to be removed in order to be free from pain, misery and sorrow? The Buddhists already identified ignorance (*avijjā / avidyā*) as the root cause of all suffering. Accordingly, it is the ignorance that has to be removed. How can anyone eliminate it? According to the philosophy of Buddhism, an individual can get rid of ignorance by clearly comprehending the truth of the nature of existence and acquiring perfect insight and wisdom leading to non-attachment, tranquillity, freedom and bliss. In other words, it is by attaining *nibbāna/nirvāṇa* one can overcome ignorance.

Then, what is the path to *nibbāna/nirvāṇa*? The answer is stated by the Buddha in his Fourth Noble Truth. There is a path, the one that is discovered and traversed by the Buddha himself. It is the Noble Eightfold Path (*aṣṭāṅga-mārga*). The eight steps of the path are as follows:[10]

1. Right views (*sammādiṭṭhi/samyak-dṛṣṭi*)
2. Right resolve (*sammāsankappa/samyak-saṁkalpa*)
3. Right speech (*sammāvāca/samyak-vāk*)
4. Right conduct (*sammākammanta/samyak-karmānta*)
5. Right livelihood (*sammājiva/samyak-ājīva*)
6. Right effort (*sammāvāyāma/samyak-vyāyāma*)
7. Right mindfulness (*sammāsati/samyak-smṛti*)
8. Right concentration (*sammāsamādhi/samyak-samādhi*)

10. *Dīgha-Nikāya* (trs.), pp. 372-74.

Of the above eight steps, right speech, right action, and right livelihood lead to conduct; right effort, right mindfulness, and right concentration lead to discipline; and the remaining two, right views and right resolution lead to knowledge and wisdom. Perfect knowledge, according to the philosophy of Buddhism, is an insight into the nature of existence and the factors that cause craving and suffering. Perfect discipline along with perfect knowledge enables one to master the cravings. Perfect conduct in association with perfect knowledge makes one's life free from suffering and bondage. It is the life of wisdom, and is completely free from ignorance. The attainment of such perfection of wisdom is nothing but *nibbāna/nirvāṇa*. And one who attains *nibbāna/nirvāṇa* is called *arhat,* the venerable one.[11]

The Nature of Reality

The various schools of Buddhism have something common to share with regard to the nature of reality. They admit that neither selves nor external objects are of the nature of substance. Thus they completely dispensed with the notion of substance. The selves as well as external objects are only constituted by elemental forces. There is no permanence either in selves or in objects. Space and time are not the determining characteristics of selves or objects, for space and time are relative to the processes which are relative to each other. However, there are differences among the various schools of Buddhism regarding the ultimate constituents of reality. There are two realist schools of Buddhism, namely, Vaibhāsika and Sautrāntika, and two idealist schools, namely, Yogācāra or Vijñānavāda and Mādhyamika or Śūnyavāda. The Vaibhāsika is associated with Theravāda Buddhism. According to this school, the ultimate constituents of the empirical world are the elements (*dhammas/dharmas*). These

11. *The Dhammapada*, VII, Source Book, pp. 299-300.

elements are directly given in experience as the basic content of our experience. These elements are real and innumerable. This position of Vaibhāsika is called pluralistic realism. Although the Sautrāntika is associated with the Theravāda Buddhism, its aim is to bridge the gap between Theravāda and Mahāyāna. The Sautrāntika is also a realist school; yet it differs from the Vaibhāsika when it holds that our ordinary experience of objects cannot directly grasp the ultimate constituents of reality. The ultimate constituents of reality lie beyond the contents of our ordinary experience. All our experiences are only representations of those ultimate constituents of reality. The monist idealist schools, namely, Yogācāra and Mādhyamika, do not accept the position of the realist schools. According to Yogācāra, consciousness alone is real and independent. It is the storehouse *(ālayavinnāna/ālayavijñāna)* of all our experiences. All other things have reality only relative to consciousness. The Mādhyamika School holds that all the elements are relative. The quest for the ultimate constituents of reality is a chimera. The ultimate reality is *sunna/śūnya* or void. Therefore, for the Buddhist there is no world of substance, but there is a world of processes. To deny the world of substance is not to deny the reality of the world. Even the world of processes as a relative phenomenon is acceptable to Mādhyamika School, for what is empirical or phenomenal cannot be absolute. The absolute is bereft of all qualities. Therefore it is void.

God and Soul

What does Buddhism say about the absolutes — God and Soul? It categorically rejected God and Soul. Every school of Buddhism, including the *Vijñānavādins,* who are thoroughgoing subjective idealists, took pride in calling themselves *anatta vādins/ anātma-vādins*. In a lengthy discourse with Anāthapiṇḍika, the millionaire disciple, the Buddha argued against the existence of God and held that:[12]

> If by the absolute is meant something out of relation to all known things, its existence cannot be established by any reasoning. The whole universe is a system of relations. We know nothing that is or can be related. If the absolute is devoid of qualities, then all things arising from Him ought likewise to be devoid of qualities. But in reality all things are circumscribed by qualities. Hence absolute cannot be their cause.

Buddhism is equally vehement in rejecting the notion of a continuous and eternal soul or self, which lives even after the body perishes. Nāgasena in a discourse with Milinda argued against the soul and concluded in the following manner:[13]

> It is on account of those things, the 32 kinds of organic matter in a human body and the five elements of being — that I came under the generally understood term, the designation in common use "Nāgasena" — just as due to the co-existence of various parts, the chariot is so called, just so when we talk of "being."

Thus Buddhism rejected the absolute categories such as God and soul, but did not reject matter outright. Nor did it accept the primacy of matter over mind. As regards the relation between mind and matter, the Buddha told his disciple, Ānanda:[14]

> As two bundles of sticks leaning against each other stand, so also, my friend, consciousness grows out of name and material form (*nāma-rūpa*). Name and material form grow out of consciousness. Both are interdependent. The chain goes on further.

12. Y. Balaramamoorty, "Buddhist Philosophy" in Rahul Sankrityayan et al. (eds.), *Buddhism: The Marxist Approach*, pp. 43-44.
13. Ibid., p. 44.
14. Cf., Rahul Sankrityayan et al. (eds.), *Buddhism: The Marxist Approach*.

Thus matter and mind are interdependent. There is no primary or secondary substance. Indeed there is no substance at all. Every substance is a process, a process of coming into being and passing away.

Rebirth and Nibbāna/Nirvāṇa

The term *nibbāna/nirvāṇa* literally means "blown out." According to the philosophy of Buddhism, there is no soul and hence the theory of transmigration of soul does not hold any sense in its case. But the questions that arise are: Does life end after death? What about the good and bad deeds committed by an individual in this life? Will they perish along with him? What about the concept of process? Life is an endless process. How can it end at a point? According to Buddhism, there is continuity in the form of a stream of human consciousness even for individual lives. A lamp fades out and kindles another lamp. A man dies. After the death, his consciousness, which is a process, enters another body. Thus the theory of rebirth is accepted by Buddhism.

The Buddha being a social reformer and a philosopher was an introvert. Attainment of mental peace is the aim he put forth before humankind. The world is full of suffering. The cessation of suffering is the ultimate aim of Buddhism. It can be attained by *āriya-aṭṭagiṅka-magga/ārya-aṣṭāṅga-mārga,* a code of personal ethics. The criterion of ethics is self-control. When self-control reaches the highest point it leads to bliss. This is technically known as *nibbāna/nirvāṇa* in Buddhism. This can be attained in this very life while one is alive. It is a changeless state of eternal rest. Thus there is a link between the ethical and soteriological doctrines of Buddhism. It is possible that the Buddha himself developed this notion of *nibbāna/nirvāṇa* more as a psychological state of rest, the culmination of his *aṭṭagiṅka-magga/aṣṭāṅga-mārga,* than as a philosophical tenet. Man can attain a state of rest, equanimity and balance not in isolation, but by discharging his social duties. A mental state of rest and balance need not be an eternal changeless state to give necessary mental peace. The Buddha envisaged the pursuit of individual *nibbāna/nirvāṇa*, and the aim of liberating the humanity as such.

Social Significance

The history of humankind clearly shows that Buddhism as a progressive philosophy played a revolutionary role by preaching equality, attacking the system of social stratification of classes (*varṇa*s) and stages of life (*āśrama*s) by infusing hope into despair of the downtrodden. The metaphysical attitude of the Upaniṣads applied to the social realm defended *varṇa* system, slavery and upper class tyranny as absolute. Therefore, Buddhism raised the slogans of revolt. It stuck to its principle that everything changes and there is nothing permanent in this empirical world. Thus the *varṇa* system is also not permanent. The Buddha while giving sermons attacked the Brāhmanical tyranny, *varṇa* system, monarchy, and inequality. His heart melted while witnessing the sufferings of the poor people. When the Buddha announced his mission in life was to liberate humanity from all sorts of suffering, it had a great social significance. All the oppressed and downtrodden, the low castes, the women, the poor, the indebted looked upon the Buddha as a great saviour of humankind. The revolutionary significance of Buddhism arises from the notion of change. Thus Buddhism not only insisted on self-discipline in order to attain individual liberation, but also propagated the basic human values in order to oppose all caste and class distinctions that are artificially created by the self-centred individuals to promote their own welfare.

Morality

The philosophy of Buddhism prescribed certain moral precepts for the benefit of humankind. They are classified into: (1) the moral prescriptions meant for a *sāmanera* or a novice, and (2) the moral prescriptions meant for the monk (*bhikkhu/bhikṣu*) or the full member of the community. The former consists of 10 major precepts, and the latter 227. The novice is ought to abstain from (1) killing living beings, (2) stealing, (3) having carnal pleasures, (4) lying, (5) consuming intoxicated substances, (6) eating at forbidden times, (7) dancing, playing music, singing and watching spectacles, (8) wearing, adoring or ornamenting oneself with garlands, scents, and unguents, (9) using large and lofty bed, and (10) accepting gold and silver. These precepts are mainly intended to develop self-discipline among the individuals.

These precepts should not be taken in a negative sense. They have great impact on the well-being of the individual as well as society. Even the family morality is emphasised by Buddhism. The following are some of the most important precepts of family morality:

1. One should not associate with the stupid. One should always associate oneself with the wise. One must honour those who are worthy of honour. This is the great blessing.
2. One must learn any art to be skilful. One must receive full training in one's own discipline. One must always utter pleasant words.
3. One must treat well one's parents, and love one's wife and children.
4. One must be respectful, humble, contented and grateful. One must listen to the *dhamma/dharma* from time to time to honour the values of the time.

The Buddhist morality seems to be heteronomous, but not autonomous as it is usually understood to be. In the first place:[15]

> No one can think out his own moral code a priori, in entire independence of his environment. It is absolutely impossible for anyone to remain unmoved by the external moral influence which is constantly working upon him. His moral ideal in the main will be the outcome of blending together maxims, traditions, customs, and ideas prevailing in the society in which he has lived, and of moral principles which he has formed for himself through the power of reasoning more or less independent of his environment.

In the second place, a community, school, or sect, which is founded on common philosophical beliefs or moral principles, would naturally require a particular moral training or education. Therefore, every system has its own peculiar moral teachings founded on its fundamental principles. What we call the Buddhist precepts or instructions are mainly intended for the training or education of the monks or lay members of the Buddhist community. No one will deny the necessity of such training or education for moulding them, so to speak, into the Buddhist type. Although these precepts are very subtle in some respects, they are nothing but the general guidelines to show the direction in which the Buddhist ought to turn on his way to final salvation. This training or education, in one sense of the term, continues throughout life. Another important feature of the Buddhist ethics is its practicability. The practical nature of the Buddhist morality is conspicuous in its teachings. As rightly held by Charles Eliot:[16]

> Argumentative as the Buddhist *suttas/sūtras* are, their aim is strictly practical, even when their language appears scholastic,

15. H. Rashdall, *The Theory of Good and Evil*, Oxford: Oxford University Press, 1907, vol. II, p. 154.

16. Charles Eliot, *Hinduism and Buddhism*, London: E. Arnold & Co., vol. I, 1921, p. 183.

and the burden of all their ratiocination is the same and very simple.

The Moral Law

Now the question that arises is: What is the philosophical basis of the moral law in Buddhism? This is the most important question to be answered. This question can be answered in a religion that accepts the existence of God, divine revelation and free will. The moral law in any religion proceeds from the divine will, and it is left to the individual to obey it or not. If he obeys it he is rewarded with salvation. But it is not all that easy to explain the source of a moral law outside the will of a personal God. This is the reason why Kant developed his doctrine of "Categorical Imperative," that is, of the will which is deep seated in the innermost recesses of human soul and which is a hidden spring, as it were, of all the moral attainments of man. The orthodox brāhmaṇas also had doctrine of their "Categorical Imperative" — of the will which made it obligatory for the people to carry out religious injunctions and accomplish good deeds irrespective of any divine will. But they saw its source in their holy writing the "words" — to which they attributed a supernatural, beginning-less existence.

All these doctrines presuppose the existence of the soul or personality and free will. In the philosophy of Buddhism, contrary to the above position, there is neither freedom nor personality itself that would have been responsible for its actions. On this question, there is an interesting dialogue between a Buddhist and a representative of an orthodox Indian philosophical system Vaiśeṣika, which defends the existence of soul and free will. The latter asks: If there is no soul or self at all, who, then, performs actions, who bears responsibility for these, and who receives the result? The Buddhist replies by asking a counter question: And who, according to you, is this person responsible for the acts — this agent? "The agent," says the Vaiśeṣika philosopher, is one who is endowed with free will. For instance, we observe in our day-to-day lived world that some person, say Bhīma, by his free will eats, washes, fights, or goes for a walk whenever he pleases. But, who, then, is this Bhīma himself, to whom you attribute the capacity of free actions? If you assume that his soul or self is free, its existence does, in no way, stand proved. If, however, by the conventional name, Bhīma, is meant the totality of mental phenomena or elements, such an agent is far from free. There are, generally speaking, three types of actions. They are: physical actions, speech-acts, and thoughts. As regards the physical and verbal actions, they are not free for they are dependent on thought. But the thought too is not free in its words and actions as it, in its turn, is dependent on its own causes — its past. And if thought itself is not free there is no freedom anywhere. All that lives and moves is under their inexorable power of causes and their effects. In these causes we do not find any acting soul or self; therefore it does not have a free will. If we ascertain soul among the causes that result in a certain phenomenon, we can conventionally call it an "acting personality." But we cannot even conventionally thus speak of a soul, for we do not find any action of the slightest consequence proceeding from it.

In the Buddhist philosophy to build a moral law by negating the soul or self and free personality would appear still more difficult than to build it without God. The Buddha regarded the establishment of a moral law as his main task. The entire theoretical philosophy of Buddhism is only a preamble to the moral philosophy which leads to *nibbāna/nirvāṇa*. The acknowledgement of the existence of soul and human personality, in the opinion of the Buddha, not only helped in establishing the moral law, but also constituted the main obstacles for it. In the rejection of the soul the Buddha saw the main trait of his doctrine and of its superiority over all others. Where there is personality, there is property belonging to it. Where there is "I," there also is "my"; and there is personal property. Where there is personal property belonging to it; there necessarily emerges a love for it in one form or the other. This attachment to personal property is the root cause of evil. And it is the root of every personal action and social injustice. Thus, by negating the existence of the soul, Buddhism provides us with a profound philosophical basis for the negation of the right to personal property. What kind of personal property is possible where there is no personality? Therefore, a real Buddhist is one who renounces the personal property and not merely property, but also family, home, and so on.

The rejection of the soul can easily lead a philosophically uninitiated mind to moral indifference. The existence of the soul, as is known, is also denied by the materialists. The materialist doctrines of Cārvāka preached an unrestricted enjoyment of life and accepted no moral obligations or retribution for one's actions. Like the doctrine of the materialists, there existed another doctrine advocated by one Gosāla Magaliputta, a contemporary of the Buddha. According to him, everything that exists — is, and that is not — is not. Accordingly, he held that there is nothing invisible and there is no world after death. Whatever a person might do has no consequence for the soul either in this life or in future, which generally speaking does not exist. The Buddha declared that of all the numerous doctrines, this one was the most foolish. He was obviously referring to the doctrine advocated by Gosāla. The Buddha held that there are actions and consequences of actions. But these actions and their consequences cannot be attributed to any personality. In his sermons to avoid the misunderstandings he took recourse to various methods. The Buddha saw all the wounds that the sharp teeth of the dogmatic faith in personality and property could inflict. At the same time, he also saw the danger of falling in the domain of non-responsibility for actions. If the humanity sticks to the idea of existence of the eternal soul, it will writhe with wounds inflicted by the sharp weapon of dogmatism. To avoid misunderstanding, the Buddha often preferred to evade a direct answer when he saw his interlocutor was not adequately prepared for a proper comprehension of the doctrine of elements of existence and of their impersonal development. Thus, when a brāhmaṇa asked whether the conception of a living being would agree with a living body or whether there is some difference between them, the Buddha gave no answer and later explained his silence like this:[17]

> Had I said that there was a soul, this would have been an untruth, for, in all elements of existence, there is none which would correspond to the idea of the eternal soul. Similarly, had I said directly that there was non-soul, the unfortunate brāhmaṇa might still have fallen into a false position. He might have thought, earlier I had a soul, but not now. When you say that there is a soul, you are always subjected to the danger of being misunderstood that there is a real eternal soul. If you straightaway say that there is no soul, this entails another risk, namely, the people may think that there is no moral responsibility for one's actions.

This very mode of speaking with reservations was also employed by the Buddhists of the later period. The famous dialogue between the mighty Greek king Menander and the Buddhist elder Nāgasena on this subject takes the following form. The king came to the old man and asked: "Is there any difference between the conceptions of a living body and a living being? Give me a frank answer." The Buddhist elder

17. Charles Eliot, *Hinduism and Buddhism*, London: E. Arnold & Co., vol. I, 1921, p. 183.

Nāgasena replied: "The Buddha himself has not given any answer to his question." The king said, "I am not concerned with the answer of the Buddha; but I want an answer from you." The elder still evaded the answer and put a counter question to the king. He asked the king: "Can you tell me whether the fruits of the mango tree in your courtyard are sweet or sour?" The king replied that there was no mango tree in his courtyard. The old man still persisted. Then the king replied: "how can I say that the fruits of a non-existent mango tree are sweet or sour?" Then the old man replied, "similar is the case with the living being or soul. How can I say anything about it when it does not exist?"

When the Buddha addressed laymen, he preached them in a most simple manner to strive after moral perfection. It is, therefore, difficult even to notice anything specifically Buddhist in his sermon. Life is only suffering. Every joy is also a form of suffering, because it is attained with effort and labour. This is the First Noble Truth. The Second Noble Truth indicates that suffering results from passions, greed, stealing, and from the wish to live and use life. The Third Noble Truth is that one be liberated from suffering, namely, the path to salvation. The Fourth Noble Truth is that there is a right path that leads to salvation. The various steps involved in the path have already been mentioned. These four Noble Truths, in their popular form, can be extended to the domain of medical science. Medical science has its own doctrine of suffering in which an individual suffers from sickness. His sickness has causes. These causes of sickness can be eradicated. Medical science looks for the ways and means by which these causes can be eradicated so that the individual is freed or liberated from the sickness. According to the philosophy of Buddhism, suffering constitutes all those sources whose actions constitute the content of the life process.

The fact is that there are some elements of existence that

have a neutralising effect on the agitation of life process. They are primarily the elements of true knowledge and self-absorption or of concentration and thought. The philosophical doctrine set forth here serves as an answer to the question as to what constitutes the elements of true knowledge. The elements of true knowledge include one's strong conviction that no "I" exists, there is nothing "mine," there is no soul, and that there exists only the world of change. This element is inherent in every form of cognition. This is simply the fact of understanding.

Buddhism as Philosophy

According to the ancient Greeks, philosophy means love of wisdom. According to Buddhism, any inquiry into the nature of reality for the mere purpose of knowing more about it is not a fruitful exercise. Mere love of wisdom is of no use. One must lead the life of wisdom. The Buddha's teachings are exclusively concerned with showing the way to salvation. In a way, the ethics of Buddhism paves the way for its soteriological doctrines. Buddhism as a philosophy is a form of dialectical pragmatism with a psychological turn. Its intensely practical approach is seen from its moral precepts aimed at salvation. The matters that are irrelevant to salvation are given very little or no importance at all in the philosophy of Buddhism. Man, according to Buddhism, possesses five "heaps" which are technically known as *skandhas*. They are: the body, feelings, perceptions, impulses and emotions, and acts of consciousness. Anything that a person may grasp or learn or appropriate must fall within one of these five *skandhas*. As already mentioned, suffering is regarded as the basic fact of life. The fundamental philosophy of Buddhism is that all conditioned things are impermanent. Description of what is happening in the life-world is not his goal or priority. His statements are intended to bring about certain radical changes in one's own modes of behaviour and experiences connected to them. If you want to achieve this, then you have to do this. Thus the philosophy of Buddhism has a prescriptive and pragmatic character. The value of any thought has to be judged from the way in which it operates and influences one's own life. Wherever one finds the evidence of such qualities of detachment, kindness, serenity, self-confidence and so on, one would be inclined to believe that the philosophy behind such an attitude had much to say in its favour. The very survival of Buddhism as an influential philosophy is a living testimony to this fact.

At the advent of Buddhism as an important and influential philosophy, its pragmatism became even more explicit. People started rejecting anything and everything other than what is advanced by Buddhism as false. It is false because of the fact that it is said by someone else. The holy doctrine of Buddhism is like a medicine. The Buddha is like a physician. Just as a doctor not only knows how to diagnose different kinds of illness and their inherent causes, but also prescribes antidotes and remedies to cure different types of illness, the Buddha too taught the Four Noble Truths for the similar purpose. If anyone tends to isolate the statements of the Buddha from the task that they intended to perform, then they become quite meaningless, and lose all their force.

Meditation is an important means of salvation in Buddhism. The stress is the result of doing something by overt action. One must control mental processes by meditation. As a result of this the Buddhist philosophy is also impregnated with some sort of psychology. There is mixture of ontological and psychological elements in Buddhist philosophy. Apart from this, the Buddhist philosophy is inclined towards the method of dialectics. It is a form of logic, basically associated with such names as Zeno and Hegel. It stands for the belief that if you think properly and deeply on anything, you arrive at contradictions. The Buddhist philosophers always welcomed paradoxes and contradictions. By defeating thought contradictions are set free. Thus Buddhism has all the qualifications to be a philosophy worth following.

Radical Pessimism

Does one find radical pessimism in Buddhist philosophy? Does it result from the consequences of its *anatta-vāda/anātma-vāda*? These questions have to be tackled. The repudiation of everything that constitutes or attracts the empirical self has led to a kind of pessimistic faith. None can deny the fact that everything that exists in this world is only a phantom, for it is conditional and impermanent. This is the root cause of suffering. Therefore, it has to be avoided, rejected, and abandoned totally. It is sometimes puzzling that the pessimistic gloom which one reads into the Buddhist philosophy of suffering makes one often cynical. This world may be a vale of tears, but there is also joy in shedding its burden. It must be renounced. But if there is a kingdom of God to win by renouncing it, the gain infinitely outweighs the loss. In any case, the best thing that one can do with such an expression "pessimism" is to discard it and look into the problem straight.

The negative attitude of the philosophy of Buddhism to this world of objects is obviously bound up with the question of the meaning of life, and the problem of the destiny of man. However intriguing this problem may be, however unscientific it may be to concern ourselves with it, we must come to a decision on it, the entire happiness and fruitfulness of our lives depends on the answer. The views on the nature and destiny of man or on the meaning of human existence fall roughly into two groups. According to some thinkers, man is the product of the earth. The earth is his home. His task is to make home on the earth. Self-preservation is the highest law, and even duty of man. Others, however, hold that man is a spirit ill at ease, a soul fallen from heaven, a stranger to the planet earth. His task is to regain the state of perfection which was his original status before he fell into the trap of this world. Self-denial is the highest law and duty of man. Our modern civilisation supports the first view and Buddhism the second. Of course, one cannot decide these issues by means of advancing some arguments. Concerning the decisions on values one must be careful not to exalt one's preferences, personal tastes, temperament to the dignity of an objective and natural law. One should only define one's position, but should not coerce others into it. The philosophy of Buddhism appeals only to those who are completely disillusioned with the world as it is, and with themselves, who are extremely sensitive to pain, suffering and any kind of turmoil or mental agony, who have extreme desire for happiness, and a considerable capacity for renunciation. No Buddhist would ever say that all men are either able or willing to understand his doctrine.

The philosophy of Buddhism aims at total happiness beyond this world of suffering. Why cannot one be content with the happiness that is available within this world of objects? The answer of the Buddhists is that in actual practice we are seen not to be content. Physical comforts and earthly or mundane satisfactions do not make a person contented. This is a naked truth. We aspire for more and more, which results in sorrow or suffering of some sort. Therefore, the human nature is not to get contented with anything. The only remedy for contentment is the complete permanence, complete ease, and complete security. These things are not found within the bounds of the world of objects.

The discoveries made by the philosophers in recent times about the human anxiety reveal that anxiety is experienced by us at every moment of our lives, and it is at the very core of our being. According to the philosophy of Buddhism, one should not forget this. The philosophers like Scheler, Freud, Heidegger, and Jaspers held that there is an element of anxiety in the very core of our existence (being). In its pure form, as righty observed by the Buddhists, it is only experienced by people with an introspective and philosophical bent of mind. If one has not felt it, no amount of explanation would satisfy such a person. If a person realises its presence, then he will never forget it. It persists even in one's deep sleep. People only try to move away from this basic or original anxiety, but cannot avoid it in so far as they are in this world of objects. The Buddhist contends that we would never be at ease unless we overcome this basic anxiety.

Immortality

Buddhism regards it to be a sensible and reasonable thing for an individual to strive for immortality. The Buddha, it is held by the followers of Buddhism, after getting Enlightened claimed to have opened up the doors to the undying. Of course, there is a great difference between the perpetuation of this individuality on the one side and the immortality on the other. Immortality is just opposite of this life, which is bound up and inseparable from death. We keep dying the moment we take birth. Therefore, birth is the cause of death. All the circumstances that lead to death are its occasions. The act of birth or conception, to be precise, is the decisive cause that makes death inevitable. We are all aware of our perilous human condition, yet we behave as if we are eternal. This is the paradox of human life. Immortality is not the desire to perpetuate individuality that is bought at the price of inevitable decay. Immortality transcends individuality.

Imagine an individual with a body, mind and sense organs. He has name and form. All these components are impermanent. As it is held by the Buddhists, anything that is impermanent has to go. At the time of death all these things will vanish. With the death of body, one's instincts would also disappear. Thus an individual loses everything that happens to be mark(s) of identification for him. He could be born anew only if he had learned to deny all that clutters up the immortal side of his being.

Survival of Values

Whatever may be the Buddhist conception of immortality, common sense cannot accept this unworldlyness as something worthy and noble, for it is unsuitable for anyone who has to live in this world. The survival value of an unworldly doctrine is almost negligible. How could it ever make an entry into the day-to-day life of the individuals? The survival of the non-worldly doctrine is evident from the survival of Buddhism as religion and philosophy since time immemorial. The Buddhist community is the oldest of all institutions. It has survived longer than any institution. Of course, Jainism is also an exception. The Buddhist values still survive and have influenced the generations of people. The fact remains that the mighty Empires built on greed, hatred, and delusion lasted just for a few centuries. The impulse of the self-denial carried the philosophy of Buddhism, especially its ethical doctrines, forward. The Buddhist ethics has its relevance for every generation of humankind.

The overview of the Buddhist philosophy given in this chapter helps us in analysing the cardinal ethical doctrines of Buddhism and their relevance to contemporary society. An account of the issues presented in this overview, especially those connected with the ethical doctrines of Buddhism will be discussed in detail in the subsequent chapters.

2

Taxonomy of Buddhist Ethics

In the first chapter an overview of the philosophy of Buddhism is provided with a view to getting acquainted with the basic tenets of Buddhism. This chapter deals with the classification of the Buddhist ethics. Of course, it is not all that easy to classify Buddhist ethics, for Buddhism as a moral system has been variously interpreted and understood. Thus entirely different points of view emerge from the classification of the Buddhist ethics. What appears to be very important in one classification may appear to be trivial or less important in another. Therefore, it is a formidable task to arrange them in a unified or a coherent manner. Before embarking on this task of classification, there is a need to look into the philosophical and sociological foundations of Buddhism. The sociological foundations help us in identifying the existing social order and the social life led by the individuals. No ethics can exist in isolation from society. The individuals constitute a society. It is the code of conduct of the individuals living in a society that determines the nature of any society. According to Plato, the just society is that which is constituted by the just individuals; and a just individual is one who is able to control his irrational part of the soul with its rational part. The irrational part is constituted by spirit and appetite and the rational part with reason. In other words, one has to dominate one's spirit and appetite with reason in order to be a just person. If a society consists of such just individuals it is known as a just society. Therefore, ethics is of paramount importance for any society. This background helps us in understanding the ethical philosophy of Buddhism in its right perspective.

Socio-philosophical Foundations of Buddhism

The Buddha is regarded as a great ethical teacher, for his immediate existential problem is the problem of suffering and how to eradicate it. The entanglement with the worldly affairs leads one to perennial destruction and negation. The Upaniṣadic seers prescribed a return to the perfect Self (*Atta/ Ātman*), the superior spiritual ultimate from the worldly affairs that represent cosmic illusion (*māyā*). There are a few stray references in the *Tipiṭaka*s that reveal the possible belief of the Buddha in an Absolute. But the evidence found in the *Tipiṭakas/Tripiṭaka*s clearly established the view that the Buddha was against absolutism of any kind. In his Doctrine of the Dependent Origination, the Buddha starts with the basic element or factor called ignorance (*avijjā/avidyā*). It is possible to argue that this monumental power of ignorance postulates the eventual, although remote, presence of some spiritual and truthful being. But it appears that in original Buddhism, ignorance is not treated as a cosmic power of creative becoming as found in the metaphysics of Advaita Vedānta of Śaṅkara, but is only a subjective non-awareness of the four Āryan truths (*āriya sacca/ārya satya*) about the existence and removal of suffering in this world of becoming. Since the force of ignorance is not a cosmic power of illusory creation, it is not possible to say that original Buddhism is a philosophy of illusionism. If *nibbāna/nirvāṇa* could mean the absolute extinction of all manifested phenomena, then it could have been possible to say that original Buddhism is illusionism. But it is not the case. Therefore, it can be safely concluded that the original form of Buddhism is neither absolutism nor illusionism.

The philosophy of Buddhism has been turned into a kind of religious sect by the followers of the Buddha. But it remained as a religion without any commitment to transcendent or cosmic God or Godhead. The monotheistic religions preach obedience to God and devout faith in a great personal anthropomorphic godhead. There cannot be any organised religious system and belief without godhead, because the basis of religion is the ejection of the temptations of the lower selves for the sake of the realisation of some superior realm of being. The Buddha openly ridiculed the existing theistic conceptions of his time. Thus early Buddhism is the only religion which is constructed on the basis of the negation of the godhead.[1] Sometimes it has been mentioned that the silence of the Buddha about metaphysical questions was an indirect indication of his views on the non-comprehensibility of superior truth by the ordinary intellect. According to Gandhi, the purity and perfection of the personal life of the Buddha are enough to confirm his belief in a supreme divine principle. But, the views expressed in the early Buddhist scriptures are consciously marked by the absence of any devout fervour for the majesty and providence of God that we find in the *Ṛgveda* or in the *Old Testament.* Thus early Buddhism poses a serious problem to philosophy of religion. For the consummation and perfectibility of the religious life what is needed is not merely a primordial God as pure activity or a God as the foundation and guarantee for a moral life but strict self-discipline to follow a moral path.

Religion is postulated on the acceptance of a God who is all merciful and compassionate and who can make responses to a life of devout communion. The theistic view of the world alone can make the world meaningful for a sensitive soul

1. W.B. Selbie, *The Psychology of Religion*, Oxford: Clarendon Press, 1923, pp. 109-10. Also see, C.C. Josey, *The Psychology of Religion*, New York: Macmillan & Company, 1927, pp. 57, 64.

repelled by the transitory and temporal character of the worldly phenomena. If there is no feeling of responsive divine communion and fellowship and no assurance of infinite immortality, there can be no religious life. A materialist, a sceptic or a nihilist could criticise some of the degenerations of the theistic conceptions of the pre-Buddhist India. But, in spite of some truth in these criticisms, it is to be stated that no system of religious faith and discipline could be found in an atheistic world. We can have social and moral rules to organise our social relations in the absence of God, but it is absolutely meaningless and futile to plead for a religious life of inner fellowship in the absence of God. Religion without God may sometimes be a mockery of words and a supreme example of self-deception. Hence in spite of great veneration for the personality and lofty character of the Buddha, the early Buddhism cannot be regarded as a religion in the sense in which we treat Christianity, Islam, Judaism and so on as religions.[2] Although the early Buddhism is not considered to be a religion in the traditional sense of the term "religion," it is deemed to be a religion in the sense of teaching a transcendence of the passions of the empirical ego and affirming the mystical quest for the raptures of contemplation (*paññā / jñāna*). Its elevated code of austere morals and its emphasis on the obliteration of sorrow and deliverance (*vimutti/vimukti*) from all pain also impart to it the character of a religion. If one refuses to call Buddhism a religion, there is nothing wrong in calling it Buddha *dhamma/dharma*. Buddhism is essentially a way of life. It is not a philosophy about life. At the same time we cannot simply say that Buddhism is bereft of philosophy for as a way of life it presupposes a philosophy.

It is also held by many a thinker that the Buddha was

---

2. C.P. Tiele, *Outlines of the History of Religion*, London: Turbner & Company, 1877, p. 137.

opposed to metaphysics because he was preoccupied with the problems of immediate release from the world of suffering. The Buddha's emphasis on the healing of a wound caused by an arrow but not dialectical discussions about the structure of the arrow is supposed to indicate his pragmatic and existential concerns. He was not a pragmatist in the sense of stressing the factual contents of concrete sensuous experience. The temper of the Buddha was absolutely and permanently permeated with the sense of complete detachment. The problem of the Buddha is personal and eternal. He was completely disillusioned with the world of becoming, for it is transient. Although the problem of the Buddha has its origin at the psychological level, it is eternal in the sense that death, disease, dismay, and final disaster are in the permanent destiny of all human beings. Modern phenomenologists, Freudians, existentialists, and neuropsychologists also substantiate the viewpoint of early Buddhism in their stress on a fundamental "anxiety" as the impelling basis of man's existence.

The Buddha discovered a way of escape from the suffering in the theory and practice of the negation and neutralisation of the human ego. The ego is the root cause of all anxieties, neuroses, impeded impulses, deviant and psychopathic behaviour, and compulsive striving proceeding from the unconscious. Hence the Buddha wanted the elimination of the ego. There is no apparent causal connection or any other relation between the pursuit of an ascetic way of life and the ever-mighty fact of death. Death, like a physical demonic colossus, equally reduces the noble and the unjust, the saint and the criminal to nullity. In a theistic system, which Buddhism is not, there is the belief in conservation of moral efforts that finally results in a realisation of spiritual fellowship and communion with God. The only rational connection between an austere living and moral emancipation is the psychological feeling that by rejecting the things that lead to pleasure and comforts in life, man achieves a vicarious conquest over the all-negating, all-destroying power of death. The terror of death arises from the fact that it pulverises all that a man holds dear. If it is possible for a voluntary abandonment of the things which a man holds dear, then to that extent the terror of death would be eliminated. Therefore, the Buddha held that an ascetic negation and rejection of the things and a steady, devoted pursuit of pure life are meant to provide emancipation. The uncertain and accidental character of death provides the justification of the passionate urgency with which the Buddha and his disciples pleaded with the people to accept the Buddhist way and to seek salvation.

The Buddha refused to accept the concept of the soul as a spiritual monadic substance. This point has been highlighted in the first chapter. The Upaniṣadic conception of the identification of the psychic self and the cosmic transcendent self also failed to satisfy him. The Sāṁkhya-Yoga account of the multiplicity of transparent selves did not evoke his sympathetic response. In the philosophical and sociological study of religions our basic concern is to see the message that has been promulgated with repeated emphasis. The points that a teacher constantly emphasises and the elements that s/he constantly stresses are of immense importance. The early Buddhism always emphasised the neutralisation and negation of subjectivism. It reduced the being and the personality of man into psycho-physical complex of the five elements, namely, *rūpa*, *saṁjñā*, *vedanā*, *saṁkhāra/saṁskāra*, and *vinnāna/vijñāna*. The negation of human self (*anatta-vāda*) as a spiritual and immortal principle shows the dangerous recoil of subjectivist psychology on itself. In the Vedic religion the external world was regarded as of great ontological significance and the great Vedic deities were supposed to have physical and real existence. This ontological speculation received a check with the exaltation of the psychic principle in man. The Upaniṣads preach the glories of the mighty splendours of the Self (*Atta/Ātman*) that is identical with *Brahman*, which is the originating and the energising principle of the universe. The critical and devastating attacks of early Buddhism were not only levelled against the supreme Absolute, but also against the infallibility of the Vedic scriptures and the sanctity of the ritualistic cult. The use of the introspective method attained its climax in the reduction of the spiritual self to utter nihility. This negation of subjective entity shows the combined action of the philosophical and sociological principles in the formation and crystallisation of the religious confraternity. By denying the godhead and the reality of the human spirit, the early Buddhism denied the philosophical foundations of religious systems.

Science in general views the things of the world in terms of the manifestation of some primal physical matter or vital principle. It tries to explain the cosmic in terms of acosmic. But the distinctive criterion of religion is to explain the cosmic in terms of supra-cosmic. If the physical sciences explain the history in terms of the concatenation of physical processes and phenomena, the religious spirit seeks to understand history in terms of supra-temporal eternity. The basic principle of the idealistic philosophy is acceptance of the revelation of eternity in the phenomenal modes of spatio-temporal location. From this standpoint, the philosophical foundations of early Buddhism were weak but for what it lacked philosophically, it compensated sociologically. The exalted and inspired character of the Buddha accentuated the notion of religious charisma associated generally with the personality of the founder of a religion. In spite of the Buddha's negation of the eternal and immutable principle of the Upaniṣadic metaphysics, his inculcation of the moral way and his emphasis on the worthlessness and vanity of the things of this world, the foundation of a powerful order of monastic confraternity accentuated the belief in the transcendent character of the founder. Sociologically speaking, one of the basic principles of religion is the exaltation of the founder who is looked upon as the human centre of awe and reverence. The reverence shown to a religious leader is a cardinal element in the institutionalisation of religion. Thus, if from the philosophical standpoint Buddhism tends to negativism and nihilism, from the sociological standpoint it presents to us the picture of the accentuation of the reverence for the sacred personality of the leader. The reverence for the sacred leader is perhaps a legacy from the remote anthropological past of humans.

Classification of Buddhist Ethics

The most simple compendium of Buddhist ethics includes the following five precepts (*pañca-śīla*). They are: (1) do not kill; (2) do not steal; (3) do not commit adultery; (4) do not lie; and (5) do not take intoxicating substances. It must be remembered that Buddhism as a teaching resembles Brāhmanism in many respects. The ethical doctrines of these two religions naturally resemble each other, with the only difference that in Buddhism ethics is far more highly regarded than in Brāhmanism. We find the four of the five precepts, falsehood being excepted, in the *Chāndogya Upaniṣad*. It is held in this Upaniṣad as follows: "a man who steals gold, who drinks spirits, who dishonours his *guru*'s bed, who kills a brāhmaṇa, these four fall, and as a fifth he who associates with him."[3] These are the five deadly sins of the *dvija* or "twice-born." One who commits these sins would be awarded heaviest legal as well as spiritual punishment. These four sins are mentioned in the ancient Hindu law books too. However,

3. *Chāndogya Upaniṣad* V. 10, pp. 9-10.

one can escape from these deadliest sins by means of the recital of *Aghamaraṇa* or "hymn of the sin-effacing."[4] From this analysis, the fundamental difference between Brāhmanism and Buddhism is clear. The latter, unlike the former, does not teach the possibility of release from any sin by means of knowledge, hymn, or through any divine mediation. It declares that we shall be held responsible for the sin we commit, we shall reap the crop of what we ourselves have sown in this life or in one of the coming lives.

The five precepts are generally explained in the following way. They are as follows: (1) abstinence from destruction of life; (2) abstinence from taking what is not given; (3) abstinence from fornication; (4) abstinence from speaking falsely; and (5) abstinence from drinking spirituous, strong, and maddening liquors, which are the cause of sloth. The first two of these may be regarded as guarantees for protecting one's life and property. As we have mentioned earlier, animal sacrifice was a common practice during the time of the Buddha. Sheep, goats, horses, and oxen were killed in abundance. Thus there was no kindness towards animals (*bhūtadayā*). Such a sacrifice was a ridiculous absurdity and is an unpardonable cruelty in the eyes of the Buddha. The Buddha never recognised its efficacy, for he regarded the life of every creature with utmost value. Benevolence, according to the Buddha, is not to be merely limited to humans alone, but ought to be extended to all sentient beings, who should share as much kindness as humankind themselves do. No living being must be killed intentionally. With this humane idea, the Buddha taught that one should not indulge in the destruction of life of any living creature however minute it may be. In this respect the doctrine of *ahiṁsā* of Buddhism resembles that of Jainism. The water filter, one of the monk's

4. Gautama in The Sacred Books of the East, XXIV, pp. 10-12; Bodhayana, in The Sacred Books of the East, III.5, pp. 2-5.

requisites, is used to filter water so that microbes may not be swallowed while drinking water. It is also forbidden to throw the remains of the food on green grass, because it may destroy the life of grass; and it should not be thrown into water where animals live, because it may hurt their life. The Buddhist monks ought not to go about during the rainy season, because there is a chance of trampling the grass that grows during rainy season. Such an act may destroy the life of the grass and small insects that reside in grass. Thus the high regard for life is carried almost to an extreme point in Buddhism as well as in Jainism. All that these two religions want to appeal to human beings is not to injure any living creature deliberately. Accidentally we may injure several living creatures in our day-to-day activities. For fear of injuring living creatures we should not shut our doors of activity permanently. Such an act goes against the very spirit of Buddhism.

Stealing or theft in its wider sense will include not only that of material objects in connection with which it is ordinarily explained, but that of immaterial ones too. Pick-pocketing, burglary, robbery, swindling, blackmail, are some forms of theft. There are many more.[5] For instance, the infringements of others' rights, unasked interference with other's business, the waste of time by those who are employed by private persons or corporate bodies, the negligence of one's duty, evasion of responsibility, misuse or tampering with public property, and so on, are all different forms of theft. Therefore, it is assumed that everyone of us indulges in some scale in some form of theft. Sometimes we commit a theft knowingly and sometimes unknowingly.

The third abstinence is that from adultery. The difficulty in dealing with this precept is that we are not in a position to

5. "The Ten Commandments" in *The Hibbert Journal*, October 1904 & *Dīgha-Nikāya* I, pp. 4-5.

comprehend the Buddha's idea in connection with it. There is not much material available to construct anything concrete about it. The following instance may help us in understanding this concept. One of the disciples of the Buddha, Pillola Bhāradvāja, in his religious conversation with the King Udena of Kośāmbī[6] held that the Buddha told his disciples to look upon women in three different ways. One must regard a woman, who is as old as one's mother, as a mother, as old as his sister as sister, and as old as his daughter as daughter. This is the instruction given by the Buddha to his disciples. Women should be treated with utmost respect. There should not arise any breach of faith in marriage between wife and husband. They should trust each other. It is this trust that retains the sacredness of home which is the abode of peace and harmony.[7]

The fourth abstinence is that from telling a lie. According to this precept no one must tell a lie to another in the hall of justice or in the hall of the assembly. One should not provoke others to speak falsely or approve of others who speak falsely. One must avoid all sorts of untruth.[8] This is the Buddha's admonition against falsehood. Buddhism as a philosophy of truth has no room for falsehood. It demands absolute truth as it demands absolute purity in one's actions. Truth is a final end of Buddhism as a science, and it is the final standard of the Buddhist ethics. We are supposed to be true in thought, speech, and action. A community (*saṁgha*) of such individuals who possess the qualities prescribed by the Buddha would be very pleasant to live in. Truth is thus essential for individual as well as social progress. The motive of falsehood is the desire to gain something (*rāgagati*) by hook or crook. Or it may be the product of moral weakness (*bhayagati*). This is

6. *Samyutta-Nikāya* IV, 110-11.

7. *Singalovādasuttana* in *Dīgha-Nikāya* III, p. 190.

8. *Suttanipāta* 397.

what is termed by Aristotle *Akrasia* or the weakness of the will. Buddhism regards covetousness as one of the ugliest vices, and teaches the power of truth speaking (*saccakiriyā*). It is a power as love (*mettā*) and sympathy (*karuṇā*) are.[9] Those who speak the truth are always strong. They never deviate from that. When a man is free from covetousness and equipped with mental strength as a result of close attachment to truth, he will never be afraid of speaking the truth.

The fifth and the last of the five precepts is abstinence from intoxicating liquors. This is expressed in the following form. The consumption of spirituous, strong, maddening liquors is the cause of torpidity and sluggishness. Therefore one should abstain from taking these intoxicants. Even they affect the physical and mental balance of an individual. Buddhism advises that one must be consistently vigilant against such drinks. It teaches us to concentrate our minds as a means of culture. Drinking liquors, which causes mental sluggishness and relaxation, can never be consistent with this doctrine. The five precepts constitute the basic compendium of the Buddhist ethics. They are called "the treasure of virtue" (*satdhana*).[10] The perfect observance of those precepts is said to be the success in morality (*satsampada*). Those who observe them would live a life of a householder with self-possession (*viśārada*) and will never meet with the king's wrath and punishment.[11] Their reputation would spread all over the world. After death they would be reborn in the heavenly world.[12] In the first place, the person who is strong in virtue acquires great wealth through his industry. His entry into any society would be permissible. He is honoured everywhere.

9. *The Sacred Books of Buddhism*, IV, pp. 185-86.
10. *Aṅguttara Nikāya* III, 53; IV.5.
11. Ibid., pp. 203-4.
12. *Aṅguttara Nikāya*, pp. 35, 171, 204, 205, 275-7.

He is respected by one and all. He meets the death without any anxiety. After the death he would be reborn in a heaven.

The above-mentioned five precepts are incumbent upon all the Buddhist laymen, who ought to observe them through life, so long as they do not give up professing the Buddhist faith. Next to these five precepts, there is a set of eight precepts. They are: (1) abstinence from destruction of life; (2) abstinence from taking what is not given; (3) abstinence from all sexual uncleanness; (4) abstinence from speaking falsely; (5) abstinence from drinking, strong spirituous liquors; (6) abstinence from eating at forbidden times; (7) abstinence from adoring and beautifying a person; (8) abstinence from dancing, singing, playing music, and seeing shows. In the above list most of them are covered under the five precepts. According to the *Mahā-vagga*,[13] there was a custom among certain religious sects during the time of the Buddha to keep the eighth, fourteenth, and fifteenth days of every lunar half of the month holy. The people used to assemble on those days and preached the doctrine to propagate it among the laymen. When the King Bimbisāra came to know about it, he approached the Buddha and suggested to him to tell his disciples to do the same. The Buddha acceded to the request of the King Bimbisāra and instructed his disciples to propagate the doctrine by reciting the collection of the precepts (*pātimokkha/prātimokṣa*) on these occasions. Slowly these three days are reduced to one day, which has become a perpetual institution for monks. This is called *uposatha*.

The followers of Buddhism observe these three precepts either on all the three days or any day through day and night. But it must be remembered that the five precepts mentioned earlier are obligatory for every Buddhist to practise throughout life. But the eight precepts mentioned later are

13. *Mahāvagga* in *Vinaya-Piṭaka*, I, p. 101.

only voluntary in the sense that they would be observed only on special occasions. The observance of *upavasatha/upavāsa* or fast day was an old custom in the Aryan community. This is highlighted in the *Śatapatha Brāhmaṇa*.[14] A householder while doing fast with his wife must perform sacrifice. He believes that the gods would be visiting him a day before the sacrifice, therefore he must do the *upavasatha / upavāsa* or fasting in their honour. The *vrata* or abstinence of the householder on those days includes the abstinence from some kinds of food, especially meat, and other casual pleasures like shaving of beard, and cutting of hair. One must sleep on floor, and must observe silence during the ceremonies. The observance of *upavasatha/upavāsa* days and taking one meal a day, and abstinence from pleasures as is prescribed in the last three precepts are supposed to have been taken from the Brāhmanic custom during that time.

The Buddha was always careful not to oppose the existing customs of his time in so far as they are not against his own ideals. He did not hesitate to adopt any custom, institution, doctrine, or anything else which he thought was helpful to his philosophical doctrines. It is quite natural that the Buddha as a moral teacher always insisted on self-control, temperance, tolerance, endurance, chastity, and virtues. Moreover, the observance makes the Buddhist laymen more ethical, rather than mere followers of a particular doctrine. He is partly leading a life of a monk. He abstains from sexual uncleanness, from taking food after noon, from wearing garlands or other bodily ornaments, and perfumes. He refrains from dancing, singing, playing music, or seeing shows, and he refrains from using large, high bed or seat. All these precepts are also included in the 10 precepts prescribed for a novice or *Sāmanera*. Thus the Buddhist layman, like the brāhmaṇa householder of the Vedic tradition, must follow these precepts.

14. *Śatapatha Brāhmaṇa,* I.1.1.7; II.1.4.1.

From the standpoint of an ideal life, the monk (*bhikkhu/ bhikṣu*) is the first in the order for he has the collection of 227 precepts. The *Sāmanera* or novice, who has to observe the 10 precepts as long as he remains as a novice, comes next to the monk in the order. The *upāsaka*, or layman, whose everyday precepts are only five, comes last in the order. The layman, therefore, by observing the eight precepts leads a more ideal life following the religious man's example. This seems to have been the idea of the Buddha in establishing this institution. While giving a discourse to a woman devotee, Visākha, the Buddha said:[15]

> He (the layman) considers, O Visākha, in this manner, *arhants* have given up the destruction of life during their life; and refraining from destroying life, and having laid aside staffs and swords, they live feeling ashamed (of sin), and compassionate and sympathetic with all living beings. I also today during this day and night will give up the destruction of life; and refraining from destroying life and laying aside staff and sword, I will live feeling ashamed (of sin), and compassionate and sympathetic with all living beings. I will follow the example of *arhants* in this matter, by which my *uposatha* will be observed.

What follows from the above passage is that the *uposatha*, in which the observance of the eight vows is regarded as the most important thing, is the imitation of the life of *arhants* for one day and night. While the five precepts are moral precepts, the eight are religious vows. In observing them, and by devoting the day to the exercises of the order, the layman becomes more religious, and thereby he is closer to the ideal of the Buddhist life.

The *Dasakusalakamma* or 10 good actions, is another category of virtuous conduct, which differs from the preceding two sets, because, unlike the two others, these good actions do

15. *Aṅguttara Nikāya*, I, pp. 211-12.

not merely include bodily actions, but also those of speech and thought. They are as follows: (1) abstinence from taking life; (2) abstinence from taking what is not given; (3) abstinence from adultery; (4) abstinence from speaking falsely; (5) abstinence from slandering; (6) abstinence from abuse; (7) abstinence from foolish talking; (8) abstinence from covetousness; (9) abstinence from malice; and (10) abstinence from being sceptical. The first three of the 10 belong to the body, the next four to speech, and the last three to thought. The first four are found among the five precepts and the eight which we have already explained. The last of these four and following three make up good actions in speech. Telling a lie, slandering, abuse, and foolish talk comprise all evils belonging to the mouth.

Speech is an important faculty particularly inherent in the human beings. It is chiefly through this faculty that we are able to communicate our thoughts and feelings to others. Certainly there are many other media of communicating our thoughts and feelings such as letters, pictures, actions, gestures, countenance and so on. All these are only substitutes for speech. We may call them speech in our broader sense in so far as they can be used as media of expressing our thoughts and feelings. Speech is thus indispensable for human beings. It is good in so far as it is used in a right manner. Evil erupts only when the speech is misused although we are granted the freedom of expression. According to the Buddha, "To every man that is born, an axe is born in his mouth, by which the fool cuts himself, when speaking bad language."[16] Lying, slandering, abuse, and foolish talk perhaps comprise the most serious cases of evil belonging to speech. But when we abstain from them, we shall be free from the evil of speech.

Slandering, backbiting, as it is ordinarily called, or to be

16. *Suttanipāta*, 657.

more precise, using language that is liable to cause separation among friends, may take sometimes a form of a false statement or report concerning other's personality, or misrepresentation of someone's actions, but always accompanied by malicious intentions to rouse friendly feeling towards oneself and hostile feeling towards the other. By this act, one wishes to separate friends from one another. Also, this is an attempt to attract one or both of them towards himself. In the *Sumaṅgalavilāsinī* we find the following definition of the term. "Any language by means of which one rouses friendly feelings towards oneself and hostile feeling (emptiness) towards another in the heart of somebody else to whom the language is directed."[17] This commentary further holds that not only the slanderous language, but also the will (*cetanā*) that prompts one to utter or disseminate slanderous language for the purpose of causing rupture among friends and making oneself friendly to them ought also to be regarded as slandering.

It is evident that it is a detestable vice in itself. There is nothing more detestable than slandering a person who is free from, at least, the charge in connection with which he is slandered, for slandering is usually understood to refer to untruth. The motives that induce one to utter slanderous language against another may be avarice, hatred, envy, cowardice, or other similar malicious ones. These evil motives are not consistent with the ethical doctrines of Buddhism, which look upon them as abominable vices, and regard concord, love, sympathy, and tolerance, as admirable virtues. The vices cause separation between two friends and the defamation or injury of one who is made the victim of this vice. They may also cause the speaker himself to lose his honour, if he has had any. No positive good can be expected of him, for he is a man of vices.

17. *Sumaṅgalavilāsinī*, I, pp. 73-74.

Abuse and using filthy and harsh language is another palpable evil that belongs to mouth. The foul mouth can create all sorts of problems. In defining it Buddhaghoṣa held that: "Abuse is a language which makes the speaker and the others feel harsh, and which itself being harsh is pleasant neither to the ear nor to the heart."[18] Derision, cursing, sarcasm, scornful language that are all harsh to the ear and the heart are palpable vices. People at times may be induced to use such language because of pride, anger, envy, or any other motive of similar nature. Whether they bring evil or not, they are regarded as vices. Therefore, one must avoid them.

Kind-wordedness (*peyyavajjā*) is regarded as one of the four elements of friendliness.[19] It is an opposite of abuse. We find this among the virtues of a woman and the virtues that are to be shown towards friends and relatives. We find the most interesting reference to this virtue in the *Lakkanasuttanta*[20] where the Buddha held that in one of his previous incarnations when he was born as a man he gave up using harsh language, and spoke only such words as were free from blame, pleasant to the ear, lovely, reaching to the heart, urbane, pleasing the multitude, beloved by the multitude. These are regarded as great virtues of an ordinary man.

The last evil that belongs to mouth is frivolous talk, oral conversation which is defined as "any language which is spoken frivolously with no purpose."[21] This is nonsense or idle talk that brings no good at all to the speaker or the listener. Sometimes it may be innocent and harmless. It may not amount to the revealing of the bad nature of the speaker. But from the point of view of the principles of morality, it cannot be called a virtue. When we engage in idle talk, especially

18. *Sumaṅgalavilāsinī*, I, pp. 73-74.
19. *Aṅguttara Nikāya* II, p. 32.
20. *Dīgha-Nikāya* III, p. 173.
21. *Sumaṅgalavilāsinī* I, 73-74.

when our moral consciousness is lax, it is prone to lead us to criticise persons in their absence, and as a natural consequence insolent or even reproachable language, which we normally refrain from using in their presence, may be used. It has no definite purpose. It is a silly idle talk meant for idle people. Such an idle talk may cause ill-feeling about those who are not present. Such an idle talk is not consistent with the central ethical doctrines of Buddhism.

The last three of the 10 precepts alert us not to be covetous (*abhijjhā*), not to be malicious (*vyapada*), and not to harbour any wrong idea (*micchadimahi*). Covetousness, malice, and ignorance, (*avijjā/avidyā*) are the three fundamental moral evils of Buddhism. One should not be covetous, one should not be angry with the world, and must be free from ignorance. They are supposed to be the depravities (*kilesa*), fires (*aggi/agni*), bonds (*saṁyojana*) and the roots of all moral evils (*akusalamala*). They are not only the roots of moral evils, but also the causes of all misery of life. As long as we possess these three fundamental evils we cannot be expected to be free from the misery of life and acquire salvation or *nibbāna*. As suggested by the Buddha: "Having cut-off desire (*rāga*), and hatred (*doṣa*) you will go to *nibbāna*."[22] Or it can be as defined by the Buddha: "he who has renounced desire, hatred, and ignorance."[23] Therefore, one must completely renounce these three evils. The Buddha or *arhant* is a person who has completely abandoned them, as a natural consequence of that he gets enlightened. It is a state in which all mental evils are relinquished or eliminated. This is a sign of a holy person.

Of the three evils, the most obstinate evil is covetousness. It has to be destroyed first. This can be termed as the evil of all evils. The complete destruction of this evil of evils itself is

22. *Dhammapada*, 369.

23. *Itivuttaka*, 68.

a great achievement. By destroying this evil alone one can attain *nibbāna/nirvāṇa*. And who has conquered this evil is a Buddha. It must be controlled, suppressed, forsaken, destroyed, extirpated, root and branch. Buddhist ethics is a continuous struggle against this monstrous evil. This evil is deep rooted in human life. Imagine how difficult it would be to uproot it. But it is humanly possible to do so. This single evil takes multiple forms. The following are the some of the forms of evil. They are: desire, selfishness, egoism, lust, greed, craving, longing, attachment, covetousness, entanglement, bondage, affection, inclination, cupidity, anger, enmity, wish to injure, ignorance, and error. We have said something about covetousness, hatred and ignorance as they are found among all the 10 precepts. There is another important evil called viewing in a wrong way (*micciditthi/mithyādr̥ṣṭi*). It is almost used as equivalent to ignorance. Holding a wrong view is also to commit a great sin. *Micciditthi/mithyādr̥ṣṭi* is defined as the denial of moral retribution. The principle of causality is the basis of the Buddhist teaching, and therefore it is natural that its denial should be regarded as the most horrible sin according to Buddhism.

Now coming to the precepts prescribed to a monk — they comprise two groups; one for a *Sāmanera* or novice and the other for the *bhikkhus/bhikṣus*. The *bhikkhus/bhikṣus* are the full members of the community (*saṁgha*). The former again consists of 10 precepts and the latter as many as 227. The 10 precepts include those precepts observed by the laymen on *uposatha* days and abstinence from using large and lofty beds and abstinence from taking gold and silver.[24] These precepts are mainly laid down in accordance with the habits and moral ideas of those days. Stealing things, drinking intoxicating liquors, dishonouring one's *guru*'s bed, and killing a brāhmaṇa were regarded as most heinous sins of that time. It is possible

24. *Nissaggīya*, pp. 18-19.

that the Buddha might have included these precepts in his moral code as these were prohibited even by the laws of his time. The prohibition of eating at odd times, or the principle of taking one meal everyday is perhaps the adoption of the institution of fasting that was practised in preparation for sacrifice.[25] The remaining precepts are also found in the Brāhmanical law books.[26] Therefore, the precepts prescribed by Buddhism and the Brāhmanical laws forbidding worldly amusement and bodily embellishment, and denying the comfort and pleasures of life in some degree, are instituted on the same ground; or the former are borrowed from the latter. If the latter is the case, the Buddha perhaps thought that what is good for the Brāhmanical student must also be good for a *bhikkhu/bhikṣu*. It is subject to interpretation.

By and large, it is believed that these precepts are intended to prepare a novice for a simple life, because a simple life is ideal for any moral practice. He would not be attracted by any external material object, and fully engaged in his moral and spiritual life. Attachment to worldly objects will certainly distract his mind and prevent it from being tranquillised. Therefore, a novice has to be contented with the fewer requisites of life, food, clothing, dwelling, and medicine as they are the necessities of leading a normal life. It must be remembered that fasting, denial of worldly pleasures, and the prohibition of accepting valuable things do not lead to any self-mortification as believed by the moderns. When compared to Brāhmanism or Jainism these precepts are lenient and practicable. Nothing can be farther from the Buddha's idea as it is very clear in the declaration of his first sermon.[27]

There is another set of precepts that is not obligatory for

---

25. Katagirisuttanta, in *Majjhima-Nikāya* I, p. 473.
26. Āpastamba in The Sacred Books of the East, 1.3.11.
27. *Samyutta-Nikāya* V, pp. 42-44.

any particular class of Buddhists to observe, but are meant for all.[28] These precepts are more for monks rather than for laymen. These precepts are found in the *pātimokkha/prātimokṣa.* They are as follows: (1) abstinence from destruction of life; (2) abstinence from taking what is not given; (3) abstinence from sexual uncleanness; (4) abstinence from telling a lie; (5) abstinence from slandering; (6) abstinence from using harsh language; (7) abstinence from frivolous talk; (8) abstinence from causing injury to seeds and plants; (9) abstinence from taking meals after midday; (10) abstinence from dancing, singing, playing musical instruments; (11) abstinence from wearing, adoring, or ornamenting the person with garlands, scents, and unguents; (12) abstinence from using large and lofty beds; (13) abstinence from accepting gold and silver; (14) abstinence from accepting uncooked grain; (15) abstinence from accepting raw meat; (16) abstinence from accepting girls and women; (17) abstinence from accepting bondmen or bondwomen; (18) abstinence from accepting sheep or goats; (19) abstinence from accepting fowls or swine; (20) abstinence from accepting elephants, cattle, horses, and mares; (21) abstinence from accepting cultivated fields or waste; (22) abstinence from acting as a go-between or messenger; (23) abstinence from buying or selling; (24) abstinence from cheating with scales or bronzes or measures; (25) abstinence from the crooked way of bribery, cheating, and fraud; and (26) abstinence from maiming, murder, putting in bonds, highway robbery, dacoity, and violence of any sort. This long list of precepts is meant for one and all.

The precepts meant for the *bhikkhus/bhikṣus* are 227. They are further classified into eight groups. These are clearly listed in *pātimokkha/prātimokṣa.* They are: *Pārājikās* (4); *Saṁghadiśeṣas* (13); *Aniyatas* (20); *Nissaggīya Pacittiyas* (30); *Pacittiyas* (92); *Pasidesaniyas* (4); *Sekhiyas* (75); and *Adhikaraṇasamaṭhas* (7). *Pārājikas* are the

28. *Dīgha-Nikāya* I, pp. 4-5.

rules that involve perpetual expulsion of the transgressor from the monkhood. The offender is said to have fallen into defeat by not observing the precepts. Therefore, he is no longer allowed to live in the community (*saṁgha*). It is the heaviest punishment given to a monk. The first *Pārājika* is a rule against the sexual intercourse. It is regarded as a heinous crime for the monkhood. There is no relaxation for the monk who committed this crime. He would be expelled from the community without any reservations. In fact, the offences against women are found in the first five of the *Saṁghadiśeṣa*s, two of the *aniyata*s, three *Nissaggīya*s, sixteen *Pacittiya*s, two *Pasidesaniya*s.

The second *pārājika* is taking what is not offered, the theft not of trifling objects, but of objects of some value, objects of such value, according to the text of the *pātimokkha/prātimokṣa*, that the king would seize, slay, blind, or banish him for the theft. There is no other rule excepting the rule on the abstinence from theft in *pātimokkha/prātimokṣa*. The third rule deals with the killing of a human being. It is not merely killing a human being, but also making arrangements for killing a human being by an assassin, uttering the praises of death, and inciting others to self-destruction which amount to heinous crime. It is also mentioned in the *pātimokkha* that abortion or the destruction of life in the womb is regarded as crime under this rule. Monks are forbidden by this rule not only to kill a human being with their own hands but also to cause destruction of life of those whom they address or others, or to make it possible, by luring an assassin, praising death, or inciting people to commit suicide. As far as human being is concerned, even the abortion of an embryo that is just conceived is regarded as a crime against human life. Coming to the question of the destruction of life of other living creatures it is held in the *pātimokkha/prātimokṣa* that deliberate killing of any living organism is a crime. It is also mentioned in the sixty-first *sutta* of *Pacittiya* that one should not indulge in the destruction of any form of life. In the same text the sixty-second *sutta/sūtra* mentions that drinking water with living creatures should not be spilled on grass or on clay. Digging of the ground where there is vegetation is prohibited. This is mentioned in the tenth and eleventh *sutta* of *Pacittiya.* By digging the ground even small creatures are also killed. In the sixth and seventh *sutta* of the *Saṁghadiśeṣa*s it is mentioned that while building a hut or a large residence for monks it is prescribed that the land or site in which this hut or residence is going to be constructed must be free from dangers. Therefore, there must be ample space around the hut or building. This is in a way not to cause any harassment or inconvenience to any living creatures. It is mainly to protect them from all sorts of natural and man-made dangers. The protection of animal as well as vegetable life is of immense importance for the Buddhists.

The fourth is a rule regarding the falsehood. The greatest crime in this regard is to claim falsely by a monk that he has acquired insight into the knowledge of the noble, the supreme acquisition. Of course, there are many forms of attributing falsehood to things. All these forms are forbidden. Like theft, falsehood is also dangerous. If a person is exposed he would be punished. Like killing, stealing, and sexual uncleanness, falsehood is also a grave crime. A monk who indulges in falsehood would be expelled from the community, and further he would be damned forever. He would never attain *arahatship.*

The *Saṁghadiśeṣa*s are rules that require a *saṁghakamma* in the beginning (*ādi*) and at the end (*śeṣa*), or which require a formal meeting of the whole community at every stage for the amendment of offences committed. This division contains the rules of various types. The first five consist of monks' behaviour towards women or uncleanness. The sixth and seventh consist of the rules concerning the building or a large hut, the eighth and ninth consist of the rules concerning falsely implicating a monk by another monk without any proper grounds or reason, the tenth and eleventh consist of the rules concerning causing schism among the members of the community. The twelfth consists of the rules concerning not to listen to what is addressed to a monk according to the law. The thirteenth consists of the rules concerning the life leading that is harmful to the laymen.

The *Aniyata*s are the rules concerning the undetermined matters because it depends upon the circumstances whether they are to be treated as *Pārājika*s, *Saṁghadiśeṣa*s or as *Pacittiya*s. All these are basically the rules concerning monk's behaviour towards women. The *Nissaggīya Pacittiya*s are the rules the violation of which results in forfeiture. This is the reason why they are called *Nissaggīya*, or those which should be given up or forfeited. They are chiefly concerned with robes, bowls, medicines, rugs, and mats. The eighteenth, nineteenth and twentieth *sutta* deal with accepting gold or silver and other commercial transactions in which gold and silver are used.

The *Pacittiya*s are rules concerning repentance and absolution. It is in this division that we find the offences of the most moral nature. Lying, using abusive language, slandering, worrying monks in assembly, stirring up ill-will against a monk who is deputed on an official duty, revealing lack of public spirit, revealing selfishness, killing living creatures, showing disrespect, giving a blow to another monk, and using a threatening gesture are all treated as crimes.

The *Pasidesaniya*s are the rules concerning matters that require confession as having fallen into a blameworthy offence. The offender ought to realise his own offence and confess it. The *Sekhiya*s are the rules concerning the discipline. These rules ought to be observed. And there are also rules concerning the legal matters found in the *Adhikaraṇa-samaṭhas*. Of course, the Buddha always altered the rules whenever he considered it to be necessary. In the *Aṅguttara Nikāya*[29] the precepts are said to be 150. At the time of his death the Buddha told his disciples to abolish some of the less important precepts. Now the question remains: what are those precepts that are less important? This question puzzled the monks of the order so much. Even today there is no unanimous opinion about the less important precepts. They vary according to the customs and practices of the society in which the Buddhist monks live. Some say it is better to follow all the precepts as they are conducive for attaining liberation.

It appears that it is impossible to enumerate all the virtues put forth by Buddhism. They are analysed and synthesised in ever so many ways. What we enumerated above are expressed in a negative form. This is not so with the ethics of Buddhism. In Oriental philosophies the moral precepts or instructions take negative forms. This is a distinctive feature. For instance, when Confucius was asked by his disciple: What is benevolence? He replied that: "You should not do to others as you would not wish to be done to you."[30] In contrast to this negative expression, the Chinese sage has given a positive instruction almost in a similar manner. According to him: "a benevolent man in the hope of being established himself, seeks to establish others beforehand; and in the hope of succeeding himself makes others succeed beforehand."[31] Of course, the two precepts exactly do not mean the same. We can very well conclude that one explains the term "benevolence" from the negative side and the other from positive. In spite of this, what is generally regarded as

29. *Aṅguttara Nikāya* I, pp. 230-31.

30. James Legge (tr.), *The Chinese Classics*, Oxford: Clarendon Press, 1893-95, vol. I, p. 251.

31. James Legge (tr.), *The Chinese Classics*, vol. I, p. 194.

Confucius' definition of benevolence is the former but not the latter. This does not mean that the term "benevolence" explained by him has only a negative side. This is also understood from its positive side too. Anyone who is familiar with Confucius' teachings will understand the definition in its right perspective. Similar is the case with the interpretation of the terms used by the Buddha. The ethics of Buddhism is akin to that of Confucius' teachings in this respect.

Every negation is a determination. This view is echoed in the philosophy of Benedict Spinoza, the seventeenth-century Dutch philosopher. Stealing is a vice, and therefore abstinence from it and liberality are virtues. Using abusive language is a vice, and therefore abstinence from it and kind-wordedness are virtues. Pride is bad, and therefore giving it up and being humble are good. Buddhism teaches us to engage in doing *kuśala, puñña/puṇya, kalyāṇa,* and to refrain from doing *akuśala, pāpa, kibbisa.* The former are good, right and meritorious, while the latter are evil, wrong, non-meritorious, or vicious. It will be, therefore, a hasty conclusion to say that Buddhism simply teaches avoidance of evil actions. It also prescribed the good actions to be performed by the individuals. In a way, to be good and to do good always go together. For instance, it is mentioned in the *Mahāmaṅgalasutta*[32] that the Buddha instructed the blissful state of a householder through the following injunctions. They are as follows:

- Not to associate with the stupid, but to associate with the wise; and to honour those who are worthy of honour; this is the greatest blessing.
- To dwell in a suitable place, to have done meritorious deeds in past lives, and to have formed right resolves for oneself.

32. T.W. Rhys Davids, *Buddhism,* London: Clarendon Press, 1912, pp. 125-27.

- To have learnt much (to be skilful in) art, to be well-trained in discipline, and to utter pleasant words.
- To wait upon one's parents, to cherish one's wife and children, to have a peaceful calling.
- To be generous in giving, to act in accordance with the *dhamma*, to cherish one's own relatives, and conduct free from blame.
- To refrain and abstain from sin and eschew strong drink, and to be diligent in righteous things.
- To be respectful, humble, contented and grateful, and to hear the preaching of the *dhamma/dharma* from time to time.
- To be patient and mild, to see sāmaṇas or novices, and to have religious conversations from time to time.
- Religious devotion, absolute chastity, penetrating the Noble Truths, and realising *nibbāna/nirvāṇa.*
- A mind unshaken in contact with the conditions of the world, free from sorrow and defilement and peaceful — this is the greatest blessing.

To conclude, the ethics of Buddhism has been classified into several groups. This background is necessary for us to understand the fundamental characteristics of the Buddhist ethics that we are going to discuss in the next chapter.

3

Autonomous Character of Buddhist Ethics

In the preceding chapter we have dealt with the classification of the Buddhist ethics. In the current chapter a survey of the autonomous character of the Buddhist ethics is to be undertaken. This is necessary to understand the practical and pragmatic purport of the Buddhist ethics. For the guidance of his immediate disciples the Buddha might have put forth many precepts. Also, there are many more which he introduced from time to time during his discourses. Most of these precepts are found in the Piṭaka literature. Whosoever has faith in the Buddha must follow them with pure heart. The Buddhist thus seems to be absolutely subjected to the external laws in the form of precepts, instructions and injunctions. The ethics of Buddhism seems to be heteronomous, but not autonomous as it is normally understood to be. This point needs to be discussed thoroughly.

Rashdall holds: "No one can think of his own moral code a priori, in entire independence of his environment."[1] It is absolutely impossible for any individual to remain unmoved by the external moral influence that is constantly working upon him either directly or indirectly. His moral ideal in the main would be the outcome of blending together maxims, traditions, customs, and ideas that are prevailing in the society

1. H. Rashdall, *The Theory of Good and Evil*, Oxford: Oxford University Press, 1907, vol. II, p. 154.

in which he lives, and of moral principles that he has formed for himself through the power of reasoning more or less independent of his environment. Apart from this, any community, school or sect, which is established on certain common base or foundation would naturally require a particular ethical training or moral education. Therefore, every system has its own peculiar teachings founded on its fundamental principles. What we call Buddhist ethics is mainly intended for the training and education for the *bhikkhus* and for the lay members of the Buddhist community. None can deny the role of such a training or education for moulding them, so to say, into the Buddhist type. These precepts and instructions, though very subtle in many respects, are nothing but general guidelines to show the direction in which the Buddhist ought to turn on his way to final salvation. This training or education, in a sense, continues throughout his life as in any other religious system.

Moral Autonomy

The ethics of Buddhism suggests that the individuals have to work for their salvation through their own power. This enables them to be more responsible for their own actions both in the present life and in the future one. They have been trained and moulded through these teachings that may continue to influence them in the surroundings in which they find themselves. However, on their own part they have to struggle for their own moral improvement and spiritual enlightenment. Neither divine nor human agency could help them according to the philosophy of Buddhism. Their own deliverance would be the product of their own unaided toil. Therefore, the ethics of Buddhism, in spite of having ideal precepts and instructions, is in its foundation autonomous. Its autonomy is greater than any other religious or moral system. The reason why we say it is more autonomous because no person or system can be completely autonomous. The Buddha preached to his own disciples not to be dependent on any other person or agency for their own salvation and enlightenment. He concluded his instruction with the following words: "and, whosoever, Ānanda, either now or after I am dead, shall be lamp unto themselves, and a refuge unto themselves, shall betake themselves to no external refuge, but holding fast to the truth, shall look not for refuge to any one besides themselves — it is they who shall reach the very topmost height, but they must be anxious to learn."[2] The Buddha with his pleasing and great personality revealed to his followers a living example of high mental culture. His personality is the outcome of uniting moral and intellectual cultures, if we can consider them separately. It is both ethical and intellectual perfection. Moral improvement and spiritual enlightenment are perfectly manifested in a visible form in his personality. He taught his disciples to follow his own example, to struggle for higher mental culture and finally attain *nibbāna/nirvāṇa.*

The doctrine of *kamma/karma* or moral retribution that forms a prominent feature of the Buddhists clearly established the autonomous character of the Buddhist morality. The Buddha held that there are three erroneous ideas about the happiness and misery in this life. To put it in the words of the Buddha:

> There are, O monks, some sāmaṇas and brāhmaṇas who maintain and believe that all the pleasure and pain, that this person feels, are results of his acts in previous births. There are O monks, some sāmaṇas who maintain and believe that these are all results of creation by the Lord of the Universe. And there are, O monks, some who think that all these have neither reason nor cause.[3]

---

2. *Dīgha-Nikāya* II, pp. 100-01.
3. *Aṅguttara-Nikāya* I, p. 173.

Further he held that if as the first group of sāmaṇas and brāhmaṇas assert, these are results of actions in previous existence, e.g. as murderer, thief, adulterer, liar, etc.; they will not be directly responsible for the crimes that they have committed. They cannot but act as they are destined by their previous births. They will have to do simply what they are forced to do by their previous actions. Thus there is no freedom of will accorded to them. If as the second group of sāmaṇas and brāhmaṇas say, the happiness and misery of the present life of beings are the outcome of divine interference, the Supreme Ruler will be to blame for these offences. And lastly, if, as the third group of sāmaṇas or brāhmaṇas think, the present condition of the living beings is produced without reason (*hetu*) and cause (*paccaya*), these crimes will also be committed without reason and cause. Everything will happen only by chance, without any causal link. We shall have to wait for chances to turn up in our favour, no efforts or strivings being needed for our betterment. Such a view is refuted by Buddhism as it gives importance to the theory of causation. Even the doctrine of *kamma/karma* suggests that our present different births are the results of the accumulated *kammas/karmas* performed in our previous existences, and our present different dispositions are also predetermined and predestined by our previous *kammas/karmas*. Thus the Buddhist doctrine of *kamma* boils down to fatalism. But fatalism is not acceptable to Buddhism. According to Buddhism, we must understand that we are changing or moulding our own fate in the next birth through our actions, because we are free to do or not to do as we please, not as the first group of sāmaṇas and brāhmaṇas assert which ascribe our actions in this life solely to the *kammas* done in our previous lives. Thus there is no one to interfere with our fate, and as our destiny continues to happen regularly as we ourselves ordain it without any deviation through the law of causation. We have the key to our fate in our own hands throughout our repeated births.

Improvement or progress, degeneration or decay, ascent to heaven or descent to hell, and happiness or misery are all the results or products of our own deeds. We ourselves mould our own fate. Others cannot be blamed for our misery and praised for our happiness. It is quite clear from these arguments that the ethics of Buddhism emphasises the freedom of the will. Thus autonomy is the most distinctive feature of the Buddhist ethics.

Moral Pragmatism

Another important feature of the Buddhist ethics is its practicability. Its applied nature is going to be discussed in a separate chapter. In Buddhism, there is no demarcating line between ethical theory and moral practices. Any theory is valuable and regarded as important provided it has practical application to social life. The former always presupposes the latter. The theory without any practical consequences is only an utopia. In the case of spiritual enlightenment, personal experience is a very important factor. When a thirsty man finds a well of drinking water, but not a rope and bucket to draw the water from it he feels that it is as good as not finding the water. Similar is the case with any theory. If it is impracticable, then one must ignore it. Therefore, the most important thing that is associated with the enlightenment is personal experience. This is true of the Buddhist ethics. Mere knowledge of any doctrine is of no value. The doctrine must be translated into a concrete reality.

The practical nature of the Buddhist ethics is conspicuous especially in its primitive period of development, when the disciples of the Buddha flocked around for the purpose of practising *brahmacarya* under his guidance. The Buddha did not encourage any metaphysical speculations, rather he gave importance to practical aspects of human life that have immediate relevance for healthy life. The monk Malunkya, the wandering ascetic Vacchagotta, the monk Cunda are all warned against their metaphysical queries. Malunkya views that man can be made purer through philosophical views (*ditti*) is also refuted as wrong.[4] It is held in the *Suddatthakasutta*, which is poetical in its expression, that there is no purification without following the eightfold path. To quote Charles Eliot in this context: "Argumentative as the Buddhist *sutta*s are, their aim is strictly practical, even when their language appears scholastic and the burden of all their ratiocination is the same and very simple."[5]

Of course, the critiques like Kern label the Buddha as a sophist, for he set aside the questions concerning the existence of personality and the like. They are not even entertained by the Buddha.[6] According to the Buddha, the discussions concerning speculative matters are of no use from the strict practical point of view. Therefore all such discussions must be avoided. But on one occasion the Buddha happened to say that he sees a certain person born in hell after his death.[7] At the same time he urged his disciples not to enter into discussions of any sort that are not practical and profitable. As regards the declaration of a certain person's fate after his death, it only reveals the omniscience of the Buddha. His omniscience and his practical attitude are two sides of the same coin.

We have already indicated the practical nature of the Buddhist ethics. In fact, primitive Buddhism as a religion was highly moral. Its morality is of a remarkable practical nature. This is what we are going to discuss in the present work. In

---

4. *Suttanipāta*, pp. 839-40.
5. Charles Eliot, *Hinduism and Buddhism*, vol. 1, p. 183.
6. H. Kern, *Manual of Indian Buddhism*, Straussburg, 1896, p. 54.
7. *Samyutta-Nikāya* II, p. 232.

the previous chapter we have already shown the relations of the virtues and vices presented in the Buddhist literature. Now we have to change our plan in order to construct a new classification of Buddhist ethics according to the modern approach. This would make the ethical doctrines of the Buddha more clear and relevant. Also, it would be absolutely necessary to see how far an ethical doctrine which was introduced some 24 centuries back is relevant to the contemporary times. With this end in view some very important ethical principles are selected for our discussion. Some of them are: self-restraint, temperance, contentment, patience, reverence, gratitude, toleration, veracity, and righteousness. They would be taken up for discussion in due course. Of course, these ethical principles do not exhaust the entire ethical system, but only help us in understanding the key issues related to Buddhist ethics. Most of the moral precepts are understood as duties to be performed by the individuals for their own well-being as well as for the well-being of the community as a whole. Thus there is no demarcating line drawn between the virtues of one person and the other. All the self-regarding virtues are social duties.

The Mahāyāna school of Buddhism levelled a serious charge against the Hīnayāna as being a school of self-interest. But it is not clear whether the southern or Pāli school of Buddhism represents the Hīnayāna or not, but it is understood as belonging to the Theravāda branch, we may conclude that it is to be included in the Hīnayāna school. The Theravāda and Mahāsāṁgika schools are the two fundamental branches of Buddhism. The charge is that the followers of the Hīnayāna think solely for their own good by ignoring the good of others. In a nutshell, they are self-centred people. They only entertained self-regarding virtues at the cost of other-regarding ones. Their sole motto is to safeguard their own culture and to attain salvation. This is not really so. In fact, all the self-regarding virtues lead to other-regarding virtues. Before transforming the society one must transform oneself.

The Mahāyāna Buddhists always treat the votary of the vehicle of the *śrāvakas* or of *Pratyekabuddhas*, in contrast with the votary of the vehicle of *bodhisattva* or of the Buddha, as a small-minded, low-disposed, selfish fellow. A clear contrast between these two types is very vividly discussed in the *Saddharmapuṇḍarīkasūtra*, one of the chief authorities of the Mahāyāna school. The Buddha narrates a story to the Bodhisattva Mañjuśrī to explain him the sorts of associations that a *bodhisattva* must avoid. Among many others it is said he ought to avoid conceited persons who have settled themselves on the Vinaya and Āgama, and monks who follow the precepts of the *arhat*. He shows that men of the Hīnayāna are to be classed together with outcastes, drunkards, heretics, immoral men, and the like. Then the story goes on to say he receives all who come to hear his sermons with benevolence, and he refrains from entering upon a dispute. But if he is asked a question, he answers not in the way of those who follow the vehicle of *śrāvakas*.[8]

In a way it is held that the two prominent schools of Buddhism, namely, Mahāyāna and Hīnayāna, are said to represent liberal and conservative Buddhists respectively. The followers of Hīnayāna are branded as a sect of self-seekers, in opposition to the followers of the Mahāyāna who are altruistic in their deeds. Of course, this is not an agreeable schism. It may be true that the primitive Buddhists had *arahatship* as their sole objective, while the Buddhists of the later times sought the Buddhahood in which altruistic dispositions and actions predominate. The career of a *bodhisattva*, a candidate for the Buddhahood, is conspicuous by his noble spirit and self-sacrificing deeds. The *bodhisattva* is one who always regards the

8. *Saddharmapuṇḍarīkasūtra* in The Sacred Books of the East, XXI, p. 269.

salvation of the others as more important than his own. But an *arhan* is more interested in his own salvation rather than his fellow beings. The Buddha always advised his monks who were *arhans* to regard others' good or salvation as highly as their own. This is mentioned in one of the Piṭakas. The message of the Buddha is: "the good, welfare, and advantage of the multitude or the world, and the good and welfare of gods and men"[9] is of primary concern.

In fact, the Buddha classified people into four groups on the basis of their life in relation to other people. The first group of people does not bother about themselves and others. The second group is interested solely in the good of the others. The third group is interested solely in their own good. And the fourth group is interested in their own and others' good. The Buddha equates the last group of people, who he regards the highest and the noblest of the entire humankind, with ghee (*sappi*) which is the most delicious product of milk.[10] As regards the five items, namely, morality, tranquillity, knowledge, emancipation, and insight into the knowledge of emancipation, the Buddha held that there are four classes of people. The first class of people keeps or cultivates all of them by themselves, but does not advise them to others. The last class of people not only cultivates them but also advises others to follow them. In this case the Buddha did not utter any words of appreciation or deprecation, but valued the last class of people the most.[11] To quote:

> Of two persons who know the gain and the doctrine, and who act in accordance with the doctrine, one who acts aiming solely at his own good but not at others' is blameworthy on that account, while one who acts aiming both at his own and others' good is praiseworthy on that account.[12]

9. *Aṅguttara-Nikāya* III, p. 355.
10. Ibid., II, p. 95.
11. Ibid., III, pp. 12-14.
12. Ibid., IV, p. 118.

When the Buddha sent out his disciples to go about preaching the doctrine and converting people, he told them:

> Go ye now, O monks, and wander, for the good of the many, for the welfare of the many, out of compassion for the world, for the advantage, good, and welfare of gods and men.[13]

As regards the help of oneself and other, the Buddha held that in helping oneself one helps another. Similarly, by helping the other one helps himself.[14] Also, a monk must enlighten a layman while the latter supports the former with material goods. Thus there is mutual dependence on each other. It is quoted by Moore:

> Both those with houses and those without houses, being mutually dependent upon each other, do exalt the good doctrine, which is securily unsurpassed.[15]

The Buddha while addressing the headman of a village held that there are different sorts of men as they seek wealth, as they enjoy it themselves, as they share it and distribute it to others. The last class of them, according to the Buddha:

> Here, however, O headman, is a certain man enjoying worldly pleasures, (a) he seeks riches through justice, but not through violence, (b) having sought riches through justice, but not through violence, he makes himself comfortable and satisfies himself; (c) he divides the riches and accumulates merits; and (d) he enjoys the riches without falling into guilt, being conscious of the danger lurking in them and knowing the results.[16]

This is an important ideal of the Buddha.

---

13. *Vinaya-Piṭaka* I, p. 21.
14. *Samyutta-Nikāya* V, p. 169.
15. J.H., Moore, *Sayings of Buddha,* Oxford: Oxford University Press, 1925, p. 125.
16. *Samyutta-Nikāya* IV, pp. 332-36.

It is made clear from our side that the primitive Buddhists were not told merely to mind their own good and welfare but also were urged to regard others' good and welfare with the same vigour. It is held in the *Dhammapada*: "Let him admonish, let him teach, let him forbid what is improper."[17] At the same time, "let each man direct himself first what is proper, then let him teach others."[18] This is absolutely necessary for a healthy community. Such individuals are a great gift to a community.

Now let us concentrate on those important ethical precepts that concern everyone. We have already listed them. Each of them would be taken for detailed discussion.

Self-Restraint

Self-restraint or self-control is regarded as the greatest virtue by many religious and ethical doctrines. For instance, in Christianity, Brāhmanism, and Confucianism, self-restraint is part of self-discipline. In the Pāli Piṭaka we find that this virtue is taught in many ways. To mention some of them, *indriyeṣu guttadvārata* or guarding "the doors of the senses,"[19] *rakkhitamanasano* or protecting one's own mind,[20] *vijitindriyo* or a man who conquered his senses,[21] *danto santo niyata* or one who is controlled or calmed, and restrained,[22] *bhavitaḥ cittaḥ* or a mind which is trained,[23] *samvuto pātimokkhasmiḥ* or a man who has restrained himself by means of *pātimokkha/prātimokṣa*.[24]

17. *Dhammapada*, p. 77.
18. Ibid., p. 158.
19. *Samyutta-Nikāya* II, p. 218.
20. *Suttanipāta*, p. 63.
21. Ibid., p. 250.
22. *Dhammapada*, p. 142.
23. *Aṅguttara-Nikāya* I, pp. 5-6.
24. *Suttanipāta*, p. 340.

These sayings are directly or indirectly concerned with self-restraint. There are many other words of similar derivation and significance that are used to denote this virtue. This fact simply testifies its significance in Buddhist ethics.

If anyone is perfectly trained in this virtue, he may be called a perfect Buddhist. The Buddhist virtues are all unified in this virtue. We cannot hold that temperance is a virtue and we have to attain it as Aristotle said. Self-restraint in Buddhism has a wider sense than that of temperance in Aristotle's ethics. Self-restraint is the starting point for the cultivation of the Buddhist morality. It is both middle and end of it. To be an ideal Buddhist one must not deviate from this even for a moment. Therefore it is treated as alpha and omega of the Buddhist culture.

Sense organs are regarded as the doors or the openings through which the evils pass to the human mind. These evils corrupt the human mind beyond repair. Therefore, it is necessary to guard these openings to check the infiltration of any kind that causes damage to the mental health. To bring the senses under one's control is a praiseworthy task. To control one's own senses and to prevent them from running their natural course forms an important part of the Buddhist ethics. The Buddha divided the assembly of monks into two classes. One class consists of those monks who are haughty, loquacious, garrulous, forgetful, inattentive, not tranquil, of confused minds, and whose sense organs are in their natural condition (*pakatindriya*). The other class consists of monks who are just the opposite, and their sense organs are very well-trained (*saṃvitindriya*). He called the former, the superficial assembly, and the latter the profound one.[25]

Those whose sense organs are in their natural state and those whose sense organs are within their control are easily

25. *Aṅguttara-Nikāya* I, p. 70.

distinguished from each other. This shows how great stress the Buddha laid upon the self-restraint of the senses. Like animals, human beings are also naturally endowed with strong passions or instincts, and naturally crave to satisfy them. Therefore, if they are not restrained by self-discipline, which is part of moral culture, and if they are left to run their natural course, the result is the moral degeneration of the individuals, and the destruction of the social order. The senses must be trained to stop any individual or social disorder. This is one of the functions that any well-developed moral system must undertake. It is true that we cannot avoid facing bad when we live in a society. But we must try to keep ourselves away from bad or evil. As Confucius rightly observed, we cannot simply be taught not to look at what is contrary to propriety, and not to listen to what is contrary to propriety.[26] We have to face what is contrary to propriety whether we like it or not. In such cases we do not have any other means excepting resorting to the controlling of the sense organs. The things outside are tempting to us in many respects, but we must try to resist them. The Buddha had all praise for a monk who conquered his sense organs. This is applicable to all the five sense organs, body and mind. It is not merely restricted to the sense of sight alone. Just as the ancient people constructed strong walls to prevent the enemy entering into their territory, an individual must train himself to control his senses so that they are under his complete control.

Next to sense organs are speech and bodily conduct. These are the two modes of the three modes of action. The mind is the third mode of action. It is mentioned in the *Dhammapada*: "It is good to restrain bodily conduct, it is good to restrain speech."[27] These are the words often uttered by

26. James Legge (tr.), *The Chinese Classics*, vol. 1, p. 250.

27. *Dhammapda*, p. 361.

the Buddha. The three forms of action, namely, mental, oral, and bodily, are regarded as the doors like the sense organs. All our actions do take the three forms of expression. They come out of these three doors. The word *saṁvara* the etymology which is *saṁ* (well) + *va* (to cover) means covering, concealing, closing, shutting, suppressing, restraining, restraint. Therefore, when we say *indriya-saṁvara*, we mean by it "shutting" the doors of six organs of sense, so that no adventitious evil may come into the mind, which, according to the Buddha's ideal, ought to be kept unpolluted, unperturbed, or undistracted. According to the Buddha, the human mind is naturally bright, but it is polluted by the adventitious depravities.[28] It is therefore wise on our part to keep a close watch on them, to prevent evils from entering the mind.

After the sense organs, it is the mind that has to be restrained from indulging in any kind of evil thoughts. In fact, if mind is restrained everything is automatically restrained. The mind must be trained (*bhāvita*), tamed (*danta*), protected (*gutta*), guarded (*rakkhita*), and restrained (*saṁvuta*).[29] It must also be directed in a right direction (*sammapanihita*), calmed (*santa*), tranquillized (*susamahita*), and brought to be fixed (*ahita*).[30] Mind must be brought to a state in which nothing can move or shake it. Such a mind is completely free from all sorts of evils, and therefore it receives the name *vimuttacitta* or the mind that is emancipated. Such is the mind that has completely acquired liberty. The eyes may see several things, the ears may hear several sounds, and other sense organs too indulge in their natural course, but they do not hold on to the mind of the individual which is under his control. Hence, said the Buddha: "O monks, you ought to

28. *Aṅguttara-Nikāya*, I, p. 10.

29. Ibid., pp. 5-7.

30. Ibid., p. 8.

train yourself as follows: My inner mind will be fixed, perfectly fixed, and no sinful, evil objects which arise will take hold of it."[31] It is a tough task to restrain the mind, but one who conquers it is a perfect *yogī*, according to the *Bhagavad-Gītā*.[32]

Like most oriental teachings, the teachings of the Buddha are subjective for it recommends us to seek the pleasures that are purely subjective and reflective. In other words, we cannot objectify these pleasures. The genuine pleasures cannot be obtained by running after objects of the world. They may be pleasant to one's eye, ear, nose, or any other sense organ, but they are only transient. They are the pleasures of the ordinary man. A mind that seeks such pleasures may get disappointed or disgusted when it fails to obtain them. Therefore we must avoid these temporal pleasures. One must turn one's mind to one's self wherein one finds the pleasures of perennial nature. Humans, like animals, try to seek pleasures through instincts. Among those are appetite and procreative desire. They may be essential for the existence and the continuance of their races. This satisfaction of pleasures does not lead to moral degeneration provided they are performed with a view to promoting one's clan. But if they are satisfied in a wrong way then they are morally injurious. The lack of reason, as rightly held by Aristotle, and the weakness of the will may result in lamentable consequences. Unlike animals, human beings are capable of rising high over their natural instincts as they are endowed with natural reason. They are capable of introspection and self-correction. The next important virtue is temperance.

Temperance

As we have already discussed, passions are abominable in the eye of the Buddha. Therefore pleasures that are connected

31. *Aṅguttara-Nikāya*, IV, p. 299.
32. The Sacred Books of the East, VIII, pp. 56, 64.

to passions must be avoided. They are: "unworthy, unprofitable, and only suitable for the worldly-minded."[33] This does not mean one should be an ascetic. Asceticism and self-mortification are against the ideals of the Buddha. They are widely practised in Brāhmanism and Jainism. The Buddha completely denounced the practice of asceticism in any form. Aristotle denied temperance as moderation of or observance of the mean with regard to pleasures.[34] Similarly, the Buddha advised his disciples not to go to any extreme. This is the only virtuous course. As rightly observed by Aristotle, the great ancient Greek philosopher, the Buddha also held that following the middle way between the two extremes is the greatest virtue. For instance, to be courageous is in between cowardice and audacity. Human beings normally seek the gratification of their desires and wants. When seeking them, they go to an extreme. This state is called profligacy. Similarly, those who completely reject pleasures of all sorts are called stoics and ascetics. Even this has to be avoided.

It is normal to speak about temperance only in relation to eating, drinking, and sexual intercourse. In fact, Aristotle restricts this term only to those three.[35] According to him, it is impossible to say whether one is temperate or profligate with regard to mental pleasures, such as honour, learning and so on, and that temperance exists only in the pleasure of eating, drinking, and sexual enjoyment, the medium of which is the sense of touch. The inborn instinct of gratifying appetite and sexual desire is natural to human beings. But they must be satisfied as per the requirement. The Buddha, on the contrary, advised people to eat moderately. It is something praiseworthy. He commended those who are moderate in

---

33. The Sacred Books of the East, XI, p. 146.
34. *Nochomachean Ethics*, III, 10, 1.
35. Ibid., 10, 10.

taking food and filling stomach.[36] Eating in excess is the sign of lack of self-control, and is treated as a vicious action. Those who eat more develop lethargy and sloth. They are incapable of any action. Their mind becomes dull. The Buddha always recommended less quantity of food and also to reduce the number of their meals.

The reasons for recommending moderate eating are many. Of course, fasting is not only regarded as virtuous religious practice, but also overhauls the body and physique. Such a practice is as old as the Vedic civilization. The attenuation of the physical body by means of fasting clearly shows that the spirit is more important than body during the Vedic times. Fasting needs spiritual and physical forbearance. The long and frequent practice of it indicates the spiritual progress. Therefore, the Buddha insisted that the tradition handed down to his fellow beings must be continued in order to subdue one's passions. The passions in a great degree are dependent on the intake of the food, especially when meat is taken in abundance. To subjugate one's passions one has to show restraint over taking excessive meat as well as food. Of course, the Buddha never advised his disciples not to take animal food. The monks (*bhikkhu*s) may receive it in the form of alms, but with the reservations that the food must be properly cooked and must be made especially for the monks. Only then they can eat it. Taking life of any living creature is virtually prohibited for any monk. Therefore he cannot kill any creature on his own, but he can very well accept the gift of meat. But the question arises: Isn't it a way of encouraging killing? This goes against the very canons of the Buddhist ethics that preaches *ahiṁsā*. The only satisfactory answer given to this question is that the aim of the Buddha is to allow his disciples to accept anything that is offered to them without any reservation. Thus there is no preference accorded by them

36. *Aṅguttara-Nikāya* I, p. 94.

while accepting the food in the form of alms. Yet, the critics are not at ease with this explanation. The monks accept the offerings without any attachment, without stupefaction, without craving, but always conscious of the danger lurking in it.

The Buddha vehemently opposed the idea of eating the human flesh in any form. It is a crime of all crimes. Similarly, he advised his disciples not to eat the flesh of an elephant, horse, dog, serpent, lion, tiger, panther, bear, or hyena for several reasons.[37] The main reason given for the avoidance of the flesh of the above-mentioned animals is that by eating it there may arise passions of ill-will. This may be the case with other animal meat too. There is an apparent contradiction in it.

As far as the habit of drinking is concerned, the intake of intoxicated, strong alcoholic drinks is completely prohibited in any form. They work on human mind and make it dull and stupid.[38] We find it included in the list of five precepts prescribed for a monk. It is also mentioned in all other precepts. In the *Pacittiya*s and *Pātimokkha* a number of references are found as regards the abstinence from intoxicating liquors.[39] Of course, unfermented liquors were allowed to be taken as they are not harmful in any way. But the orthodox Buddhists vehemently opposed to all forms of intoxication whether fermented or unfermented. Thus they put an end to schism.[40] It is mentioned in the *Dhammikasutta*:

> Let the householder who approves of the *dhamma* not give himself to intoxicating drinks; let him not cause others to drink, not approve of those that drink, knowing it to end in madness.

37. *Vinaya-Piṭaka* I, pp. 218-20.
38. *Gautama* in The Sacred Books of the East, vol. II, p. 20.
39. *Vinaya-piṭaka* IV, pp. 109-10.
40. *Mahāvaṁsa*, Chap. IV.

> For through intoxication the stupid commit sins and make other people intoxicated, let him avoid this seat of sin, the madness, this folly, delightful only to the stupid.[41]

Thus mental sluggishness and bodily torpidity are the results of intoxication. An intoxicated person develops temporal insanity. Thus he does not know the consequences of his foolish actions. Thus the Buddha recommended the doctrine of "constant vigilance" that expects us to be watchful, not only when we are awake, but also in sleep. We should be always mindful and conscious of what we do or in what condition we are. The next important ethical precept is contentment.

Contentment

It is supposed to be a mental condition of a person who is satisfied with what he possesses or obtains, or with the position in which he finds himself. A person may get or obtain more but he does not desire it. He may also improve his position, social or professional, through some medium that lies in his power, but he declines to do so.[42] There are degrees of contentment. This is a greater Buddhist virtue. In Pāli the contentment is called *santuṣṭi.* Contentment varies according to the nature and constitution of the individuals. The scarcity of what one has or gets, or the humility of the position in which one finds oneself, does not matter much for such a one. In poverty or humiliation he will find perfect satisfaction and pleasure. These are the two essential ingredients of contentment.

Being satisfied with anything which one has or obtains is a virtue viewed even from the standpoint of common sense. People normally commend such individuals. It is really

41. *Suttanipāta,* pp. 398-99.

42. *Dīgha-Nikāya* III, pp. 224-25.

praiseworthy to be contented with whatever comes to one's lot, and to covet any more. As circumstances often oblige us to do so, this is quite necessary for human life and society. We cannot enjoy perfect happiness unless we bring our coveting hearts and greedy minds under complete control. The satisfaction of material gains and greed for having more and more, depriving others of everything that is required for their minimum living is a vice. This is clear from our day-to-day experience. There are people who always indulge in satisfaction of their own desires. The first thing that we ought to bear in mind is that we cannot expect to have everything that we desire to have at the cost of others' happiness. People with such a temperament would never be happy with the things that they possess. Their greed for material property increases.

When the Buddha was asked a question by Tissa Metteyya: Who will be satisfied in this world? He replied: "One who lives a holy life in respect to sensual pleasures, and one who is free from desires and mindful."[43] Such a condition would lead to *santuṣṭi* always occurring together with having few desires. Therefore, it is natural that self-restraint as a high virtue and covetousness as an abominable vice are treated by the Buddha. Poverty itself, if it is simply nothing but poverty, cannot be said to have any ethical value. Nothing can be so miserable than the life of a poor man. He perpetually hungers for food, riches and other comforts. He is one who perpetually complains about his poor living conditions. A contented man would never do this. He is poor but he never aspires for riches, he never grumbles over his poverty. He is satisfied with his present condition. A dissatisfied or frustrated individual finds no satisfaction even in the heap of riches. No less miserable is the condition of a rich man who craves for riches after riches. He may

43. *Suttanipāta*, p. 1039.

accumulate heap upon heap, but he refuses to use those riches for himself or for others. Therefore, they do not give him any satisfaction.[44] Whether poor or rich people ought to be satisfied with whatever they have. People should not be enslaved by mere ideas of poverty and riches, humiliation and dignity. They are all concerns of relativity.[45] The Buddha explained the satisfied state of a monk. He told the King Ajātaśatru that a monk is contented with whatever he has. He requires a small piece of cloth just to protect himself. He requires a small quantity of food just to survive. He can just carry all his belongings along with him. This shows the kind of frugal life that a monk lives. He finds utmost satisfaction in that.[46] It is the same with his dwelling or other requirements of life. A monk declares about his requisites of life thus:

> Let (a monk) fetch clothes from dust-heaps, cemeteries, or highways, and making them into a double robe, let him wear a coarse dress. Let him be humble, restrained, and guarding the doors of the senses, go on his begging round from house to house in regular succession. Let him be contented even with coarse food, and let him not desire any other abundant delicate food; the mind which is covetous of delicacies does not take delight in meditation.[47]

The monks are not supposed to have any personal possessions except those few things that are essential for their daily life. This makes them free from the life of luxury and also from the objects of the world. They develop a sense of detachment. Being satisfied with whatever he possesses a monk is to lead a life of perfect self-control. It may sound strange or rather absurd if he declares that he finds satisfaction and pleasure in such condition, which is nothing but a succession of trails

44. *Samyutta-Nikāya* IV, pp. 332-36.
45. *Dhammapada*, p. 201.
46. *Samyutta-Nikāya* I, p. 71.
47. *Theragāthā*, pp. 578-80.

in the eye of an ordinary man, especially the men living in advanced and sophisticated human societies. But satisfaction is a subjective state. If a person is trained properly in this condition he will certainly be satisfied with whatever he possesses. Therefore he will certainly attain higher, nobler life. The material deficiencies do not bother him at all. In the *Dhammapada* it is mentioned that "contentment is the noblest wealth."[48] In a contented man, the good things increase and the bad ones decrease.[49] Therefore, contentment is good for the entire community of people.[50] The next important moral precept is patience.

Patience

It is another important virtue to be cultivated by a disciplined individual according to Buddhism. Most of us lack patience. This is visible in our day-to-day life world. Patience is also a form of self-control. One has to exhibit utmost patience and endurance when one faces hardship, mental suffering or bodily pain. Therefore, it is a laudable virtue. Patience takes various forms. As a matter of fact, patience, endurance, humility, contentment, and other similar virtues are cousins in the sense that they belong to part and parcel of self-control. When an individual is under perfect self-control he would be naturally equipped with all these virtues. Yet, each of them has its own value in a given situation. A moral life is a perpetual struggle in abstaining from all sorts of evils. These evils may be in the form of mental or physical conditions. Therefore one has to develop utmost sense of patience in dealing with these ills. In other words, the subordination of these lower impulses to higher forms the aim and process of moral culture. Whether it is for one's own sake or for the

48. *Dhammapada*, p. 204.

49. *Aṅguttara-Nikāya* I, p. 12.

50. Ibid., pp. 16-17.

sake of others, the morally upright man has to make strenuous efforts to practise them.

The Buddha himself practised whatever he preached to his disciples. It is mentioned in the *Ariyapariyesanasutta* that the Buddha underwent several ordeals in the pursuit of enlightenment.[51] The abnegation of the comforts of life and the struggle against human passions are also called patience. The personification of the wickedness or the evil side of the human nature (*māra*) has to be fought.[52] The Buddha's whole life is a struggle against the evil of one kind or the other. The disciples of the Buddha, both male and female, followed the footsteps of the Buddha in this regard. *Māra* is an enemy of the Buddha that tries to attract his disciples to take the wrong path. When the disciples are in the state of meditation, the *māra* appears in a terrifying figure to frighten them. Or he makes a fearful noise to distract their attention. It may also tempt the female disciples with all sorts of sensuous desires. Or it tries to create misunderstanding between the monks and the devoted laymen. *Māra* is the general of the evil army.[53] Therefore, the monks must be careful with him. A fearless monk is one who says: "Now I live keeping myself free from fear, and I can no more be affected by *māra*."[54] Once he attains the four stages of meditation he is said to have overcome the *māra*. Thus patience is the strong armour with which one can resist mental evils.

Even in our daily life one has to exercise patience to the extent that is needed for us. Pain, physical or mental, difficulty, poverty, sickness, various sorts of obstacles must be borne with unfaltering firmness of the mind. Further, one may meet with provocation, insult, threat, or even injury

51. *Majjhima-Nikāya* I, pp. 160-75.
52. H. Kern, *Manual of Indian Buddhism*, pp. 17, 20-21, 24.
53. *Theragāthā*, p. 571.
54. *Aṅguttara-Nikāya* IV, pp. 434.

against which in the majority of cases we can do nothing except being patient. If we return violence by violence, there would be no end in sight. Enmity would give rise to enmity. Revenge would rouse more revenge. Resentment could never be conquered by resentment. Hatred would only result in further hatred. In all these cases the best thing would be to show love, sympathy, forgiveness, tolerance, and so on. The Buddha held that: "The hatred of those will never be appeased who harbour ideas such as he rebuked me, he struck me, he conquered me, or he robbed me."[55]

Patience is one of the 10 perfections recommended for the *bodhisattva*.[56] It is absolutely necessary for the attainment of the Buddhahood, the highest human attainment. In one of the Jātaka stories it is said in the following way. An ascetic, who represented as the previous incarnation of the Buddha, bravely faced an ordeal. The *bodhisattva* in this case was born in a very rich family. After the death of his parents, he took up the life of an ascetic and entered into the Himalayan mountains. Then as per the custom of the ascetics he came down to Banāras and lived in the royal garden. One day the king of the country went to the garden along with his men. The king was fully drunk and fell asleep. Meanwhile his female attendants, unable to bear the boredom, roamed about the garden and found the ascetic. He was sitting under a *sāla*-tree. His composed behaviour attracted the attention of these female attendants of the king. They treated him with respect. He preached the doctrine to them. They attentively listened to his sermon. The king awoke and found his female attendants missing. Later on he came to know that they were with the ascetic. He was in fury and used foul and abusive language upon the ascetic. He asked the ascetic what his doctrine was. The ascetic replied: "Not to be angry when

55. *Dhammapada*, p. 3.

56. Jātaka I, pp. 20-28.

living among abusive, harmful, and blaming people." The king became furious and ordered his men to beat the ascetic. He was beaten black and blue all over. The blows broke his skin and flesh, and blood came down in stream. The king again asked him what his doctrine was. He gave the same reply. The king was surprised at the ascetic's patience. He asked his executors to mutilate the ascetic's arms and legs, ears and nose. Satisfied with his cruel deed the king went away. The ascetic replied to the king: "get angry, O great hero, with one who has had his arms, legs, ears, and nose cut-off, but never take wrath against the country."[57] The ascetic showed extreme patience.

Patience is sometimes juxtaposed with tenderness (*soracca*).[58] It is also mentioned as one of the four characteristics of a monk along with rectitude, swiftness in apprehension, and tenderness. A monk who is equipped with these four is said to be worthy of worship, offerings, respectful salutation, and is a fertile fruit-bearing field of the world.[59] The next important moral precept is reverence.

Reverence

It is one of the emotions that we exhibit towards persons who are superior to us in some respects, or towards objects that are religiously sacred. It is on the one hand an expression of gratitude for the indebtedness that we feel to owe them. It is a negative self-feeling. The object towards which this emotion is directed, these and other feelings, such as trust, awe, wonder and so on, in some cases blend together in it. As it is already held there is no Supreme God in Buddhism. Therefore this emotion of reverence is expressed on the one hand towards the Buddha, the *dhamma*, and the *saṁgha*, and

57. Jātaka, I, pp. 39-43.

58. *Aṅguttara Nikāya* I, p. 94.

59. Ibid., II, p. 113.

on the other towards parents, elders, wise men, teachers, benefactors and so on. In the family and social life of laymen, or in the religious life of monks, reverence is regarded as a prominent virtue. Early Buddhist literature shows how the order or well-being of the community has been established by the presence of this virtue among them. It is an essential condition of social welfare. The Buddha held: "So long as the Vajjians honour, esteem, revere, and support their elders, and hold it a point of duty to hearken to their words, so long it may be expected, they will not decline, but prosper."[60] As it is an important condition of the welfare of social life in general, so also it is with the religious community. Mutual respect among them is taught as essential for their harmonious living.

Now who are those worthy of reverence, honour, and respect? Of course, the Buddha, the *dhamma/dharma,* and the *saṁgha* are the first holy objects of respect and reverence. To be a Buddhist this is mandatory. The Buddha is the head of the community and as the perfect ideal embodiment of morality and knowledge is the highest revered of the three. Whether the Buddha is alive or dead he is the first to be revered. Although in the early part of Buddhism, the human side of the Buddha's personality was considered, later on his personality was carried to the degree of deification. He in his simplest capacity was only a moral teacher, fully self-controlled, fully purified, fully enlightened, and therefore endowed with perfect knowledge and goodness. The Buddha is an *arhan*, fully awakened, perfect in knowledge and demeanour, he is well-attained. He has the knowledge of the world. He is the supreme leader of men willing to be liberated or awakened.

What made the Buddha deserve to receive the worshipping homage and adoration of his followers is the

60. *Dīgha-Nikāya* II, p. 74.

compassionate self-sacrificing spirit which he manifested in both his teaching and life. He is *bahujanahitānukampā*.[61] He is one who sympathetically feels for the welfare of the humanity. He is *sabbabhutānukampā*.[62] He is one who is compassionate to all beings. Throughout his long life he served as a saviour of the world. The Buddha's aim was to promote good, benefit, and welfare of the world by means of teaching which he has instituted. Therefore he is worthy of veneration.

After the Buddha comes the *dhamma*. It is not all that easy to explain this concept in a few words. It is one of the three objects of worship and reverence for the Buddhists. The *dhamma* signifies the central doctrines of Buddhism. In fact, the teachings of the Buddha are summarised in the form of the *dhamma*. It consists of the Four Noble Truths, as a means to *nibbāna*. The most important passage that explains the nature of the *dhamma* is: "Well proclaimed by the Exalted One is the *dhamma* as bearing on the present life, not involving time, inviting all to come and see, to be understood by every wise man for himself."[63] The *dhamma* ought to be revered by every Buddhist for it is sacred.

The third object of reverence is *saṁgha* that comprises a community of monks. As has been mentioned elsewhere, the Buddhist laymen must revere the monks for their self-controlled way of living, and for exhibiting social virtues that are conducive for the harmony and progress of society. The monks are known as the sons of the Buddha. They inherit the *dhamma* of the Buddha just as the laymen inherit moveable and immoveable property from their fathers and ancestors.[64] The monks are the saviours, teachers and leaders of the world. They follow the Buddha's teachings in order to eradicate pain

61. *Majjhima-Nikāya*, p. 693.
62. *Aṅguttara Nikāya* II, p. 9.
63. *Dīgha-Nikāya* III, p. 5.
64. *Majjhima-Nikāya* I, pp. 12-16.

and suffering that are the results of ignorance and sin. They deserve the same respect as accorded to the Buddha. The monks by themselves do not seek anything from anyone. A true monk is one who does not bother about praise or honour. To quote a familiar passage:

> Those who are trained well, the order of the exalted one's disciples, even the four branches thereof; the eight classes of individuals well trained in uprightness, in principle, and in courtesy. This order should be respected and revered; gifts should be to it, and homage; for it is world's unsurpassed field (for sowing) merit.[65]

A monk who is not attracted or distracted by any pleasant object, but is able to tranquillise his mind even in its presence, as the king's state elephant, which sees and hears the hostile army approaching, though struck with one or many arrows, is yet able to stand fast in the battlefield is worthy of reverence, respect and honour.

Of course, monks voluntarily must not seek marks of reverence. They must always try to attain superior morality, superior contemplation, and superior wisdom. Such monks alone are worthy of receiving honour and homage from others. A monk must extend love, compassion, and sympathy even when his fingers are chopped by the enemies. A monk is a true teacher, preacher, and a practitioner of exhortation. The most important aspect of domestic and social life of the Buddha is filial duty. Every layman must recognise its importance. Or put it in the words of the Buddha: "He who is rich does not support mother or father who are old or past their youth . . . that is the cause (of loss) to the loser."[66] Further he said: "Let the householder dutifully maintain his parents, and practice an honourable trade; he who observes this

---

65. *Dīgha-Nikāya* III, p. 5.

66. *Suttanipāta*, p. 98.

strenuously goes to the gods by name *sayampabhas*."[67] Also: "Waiting on mother and father, protecting child and wife, and a quiet calling; this is the highest blessing."[68] However, unlike in Brāhmanism and Confucianism, the filial duty is not attached much importance in Buddhism after the departure of the parents from this world. Filial duty is taken very seriously by the Buddhists. It is not imposed by the parents on the householders. It is based on the gratitude of the children towards their parents. It is developed through the mutual affection between parents and children. If parents are good to children, then children are good to parents. They become worthy of children's respect and reverence.

Parents risk their lives for the well-being of their children. They pour out everything that they have for the progress of their children. They restrain the children from vice, they exhort him to virtue, they train him to a profession, and they contract a suitable marriage for them.[69] Therefore the children must be indebted to their parents. Apart from parents, the people who are worthy of reverence and respect are old people, wise men, and learned teachers. The senior members of the society deserve honour and respect as they share their social experience and share it for the future of society. As the Buddha mentioned, grey hair is not always a sign of maturity, it only indicates the mere maturity of age.[70] A person is revered because of his high moral observance and for the cultivation of virtues. After the reverence, the most important moral precept is gratitude.

Gratitude

Men are basically conscious social beings inclined towards

67. Ibid., p. 404.

68. Ibid., p. 262.

69. *Dīgha-Nikāya* III, p. 189.

70. *Dhammapada*, p. 206.

building up a society of harmonious relations. When they get themselves acquainted with one another in the society, they develop social interaction. They start showing love and affection towards their fellow members of the society. If benevolence springs from love of fellow beings, gratitude springs from the feeling of obligation for affection, respect, or service received. The former is primary and active while the latter is secondary and passive. Gratitude arises from the sense of feeling something good or desirable, whether material or immaterial, when it is conferred on an individual by another. It is a valuable social virtue.

Humans are intricately related to each other in any society. The interpersonal relations enhance peace and harmony in any progressive society. Sometimes they are also connected to people even when they are not members of the same society due to several obscure reasons. Distance of time and space does not hamper the formation of relations. The doctrine of transmigration taught by all Indian religions, and especially by Buddhism, convinces us that the relations not only exist among men but also between men and other living creatures. We express our gratitude in some form or the other to others or other living creatures for their help in this world. Coming to the relation between monks and laymen, it is viewed as a great relation, for the former and latter are mutually dependent on each other. The monks receive the kindness of laymen. Similar is the case with laymen. They receive kindness from monks. Mention is often made of two sorts of donation — spiritual and temporal. The former is everlasting, while the latter is transient. The former prepares the individual for spiritual well-being and the latter for the material well-being. Monks on their side have spiritual gift to bestow on the laymen, and the latter have material goods to be given to the monks for their day-to-day life. It is held that:

> The disciples of the Bhagava (the Buddha) are well-conducted, they live uprightly, prudently, and properly; they are (classed collectively as) four pairs and eight individuals. The disciples of the Bhagava are fit objects for worship, worthy of hospitality, offering, and respectful salutation. They are the best merit producing field for the lay world.[71]

These venerable monks are collectively called refuge, a lamp, an object of recollection, an object of faith and worship. They are the donors of the spiritual gift, which is the best of all gifts.[72] They are the real heirs of the Buddha in so far as the spiritual matters are concerned.

Leading a life of purity and holiness, and making constant efforts to ennoble and elevate themselves, monks guide people not only through their speech, but also through their action and life of self-control and self-contentedness. They are perpetually intent on the accomplishment of their own as well as others' benefit.[73] The assistance between monks and their lay brothers and sisters is mutual. The monks serve spiritual food, their lay brothers and sisters serve the monks with material food and other requisites of frugal life. Pleasure of life in its ordinary sense is completely denied. Thus indebtedness is reciprocal. They feel it is an obligation on their respective parts. The monks have to express their gratitude to their lay brethren when they receive alms from them. The technical term used for gratitude in this connection is *anumodana*, meaning "subsequent rejoicing" or "sympathetic joy." This is nothing but taking delight in each other's meritorious deed(s).

There are not many references to gratitude or ingratitude in the discourses of the Buddha in the Piṭaka. Perhaps the

71. *Aṅguttara-Nikāya* I, p. 208.

72. *Dhammapada*, p. 354.

73. *Aṅguttara-Nikāya* IV, pp. 134-35.

following few are worth mentioning. The Buddha once explained the condition of a wicked person. He held: "The wicked person is one who is not grateful and who does not bear in mind any good rendered to him. The disposition of the ungrateful man, who does not bear in mind a good rendered to him, is the condition of the wicked person."[74] The virtuous person is one who has just opposite qualities. Therefore, the Buddha advised his disciples to be grateful to those who have done so much to us. As regards the children doing service to the parents, the Buddha held that children should not merely provide material comforts to their parents, but must serve them spiritually. That alone is counted as true gratitude. Sending parents to old-age homes and providing them with all comforts is not real service. Parents are not satisfied for they are separated from their dear ones. All that they need is the attention of children and nearness to them. Therefore, the Buddhist love is always understood as motherly and fatherly love, and the Buddhist gratitude is always the same as that which a dutiful child feels towards his parents. The next important moral precept is toleration.

Toleration

This is another important characteristic of the Buddhist ethics. The Buddha himself was an embodiment of toleration. He always overlooked insults and injuries, both physical and mental, caused to him. He always forgave his opponents and excused his own disciples when they tried to tread the wrong path consciously or unconsciously. Toleration in Buddhism is regarded as other-regarding virtue which is of paramount importance to the Buddhist ethics. One must forgive the indolence or offences of the others, but one must be strict in controlling oneself. Therefore, Buddhism is free from all prejudices or exclusiveness or even from bigotry.

---

74. *Abhidhammattasaṁgha*, p. 297.

One of the disciples of the Buddha, Sarabha, declared that since he is perfect in all the doctrinal aspects of Buddhism he wanted to quit the monkhood. The other disciples of the Buddha reported this matter to the Buddha. On knowing this he approached Sarabha and asked him whether what he heard from his disciples was true. The Buddha said, "if what you have learnt is perfect I am pleased with it, if not I will make you perfect." Such are the words of the Buddha. He never used harsh language against any of his disciples when they are found guilty of one offence or the other. He always admonished them gently for their committal. He usually said: "It is improper, O monks, what these foolish persons are doing, it is unbecoming, indecent, unworthy of sāmaṇas, unallowable, and to be avoided."[75]

The Buddha always treated his disciples like his own sons. The feelings between them were similar to those between parents and children. The same feelings continued to exist among monks. Although natural family bonds of monks are completely cut-off, still the fatherly and childlike relations existed in the *saṁgha*. When teachers rebuke the pupils, it is not a rebuke but only a corrective measure which arises out of benevolence, compassion, pity. The teachers rebuke the pupils with tears in their eyes. The Buddha was tolerant towards heretics. He had no prejudice against their ceremonies, although surely on many occasions he taught the uselessness of these ceremonies and rituals publicly. He denounced asceticism of all sorts. Many a time heretics openly exhibited their jealousy towards the Buddha's success, plotted to defame him by foul means. But they were not successful. In spite of these things the Buddha never rebuked them openly or publicly nor used bad language against them. The next important moral precept is veracity.

---

75. *Vinaya-Piṭaka* I, p. 45.

Veracity

Abstinence from speaking untruth is another important moral precept. It is listed among the five precepts prescribed for monks. It is also included in the eight precepts meant for laymen too. The Buddhists of all classes are forbidden from speaking untruth. Lying is a common practice in our day-to-day life. People resort to lying to cheat others and for petty gains. People of the primitive ages could not free themselves from committing it. Also, the people of the most civilised societies give way to it. This sin is committed by young and old, wise and foolish, knowingly or unknowingly, intentionally or unintentionally. According to the Buddha, it is a detestable vice. Lying is always accompanied by some sin or the other. Hypocrisy, treachery, dishonesty, double tongue, false testimony are different forms of lying. To cover one lie men have to indulge in a series of lies. As rightly said by the Buddha: "If a man has transgressed one law, and speaks lies and scoffs at the other world, there is no sin which he will not commit."[76] A sinful man in general is a great liar. A person who resorts to lying may commit any sin. Therefore, the Buddha sternly warned his disciples to keep away from this sin.

If lying is a sin, truth-speaking is an admirable virtue. The truth is a supreme goal. Come what may, one should always tread the path of truth. By truth we understand things as they are. In this context it is appropriate to mention about the *moha* or stupidity which is one of the three radical evils in the Buddhist philosophy, the other two are *rāga* and *doṣa*. *Avijjā* or ignorance is treated as the root cause of all evils. The Buddha always held that the truth eternally exists whether he had appeared in the world or not. The Pāli equivalent for truth is *sacca*. Therefore, stick to truth in all your speech and

76. *Dhammapada*, p. 176.

action, said the Buddha to his disciples. One of the titles that the Buddha used most frequently in referring to himself and any other Buddha is *tathāgata*. One of the interpretations of this expression is "one who has come at the real truth."[77] The Buddha is characterised thus. He sought after truth and found it. The Buddha and who followed the path of the Buddha see things really as they are. The Buddha declared that he was "making truth to cut away the weeds."[78]

As the truth is essential for the Buddha himself, so it is to his followers. It is the final goal set forth by the Buddha to entire humanity. Like other moral precepts, to cling to truth-speaking is also a great virtue. As it is mentioned in the *Dhammapada:* "Speak truth, do not get angry, and give even a little if asked; one may approach the gods through three causes."[79] In fact, the doctrine of Four Noble Truths is the sublime truth, according to Buddhism. People who entertain ambitious desires, selfish motives, and cowardly tactics indulge in lying. They expect to gain something materially though undeserving. This is the psychology of immature humans. Undue gain, respect and praise are the evils of the worst type. Similar is the case with cowardice. A coward is a sinner. He refrains from truth-speaking. His moral weakness compels him to express things in a false or dubious manner. Basically it results from the lack of courage. Therefore, truth-speaking is an important moral duty.[80] Sometimes the truth is hidden in obscurity. One must try to reach it out. It is a great treasure if one finds it. The next important moral precept is righteousness.

---

77. *Sumaṅgalavilāsinī* I, pp. 59-67.
78. *Dīgha-Nikāya* I, p. 4.
79. *Dhammapada*, p. 224.
80. E.W. Hopkins, *The Religions of India*, Boston, 1895, p. 203.

Righteousness

In the ancient Vedic literature righteousness is referred to as *ṛta*. This term represented both cosmic and moral order in addition to right, law and righteousness. According to the ancient Indian thought the *ṛta* manifests in the form of nature and its processes, and also in human society. Everything in nature and society moves as per the *ṛta*. Thus the order of nature is identified with that of human society or the moral life. And there is no untruth in the sphere of *ṛta*. *Satya* and *dharma* are also equated with righteousness. However, we do not find any equivalent Pāli word for *ṛta* or righteousness in the Buddhist literature. In fact, the expression *dhamma* served the purpose. Of course, it is used in immense variety of senses by the Buddhists. In Pāli Piṭaka the word *dhamma* stands for the following shades of meaning. They are as follows:[81]

1. Things of objective existence, phenomenal objects; conditional, composites;
2. Mental, moral, physical states of the individual, condition of life;
3. Having the nature of being subject or liable to;
4. Custom; duty; rule; ordinance; law; and
5. The Buddha-*dhamma*, implying roughly the following different meanings:
    a. General name of the Buddha-*dhamma;*
    b. One part of it, the other being Vinaya, if divided into two, or Vinaya and *Abhidhamma*, if divided into three;
    c. One of the three Buddhist holy objects, the other two being the Buddha and *saṁgha* or community;

81. T.W. Rhys Davids, *Buddhism*, London, 1896.

d. The truth attained to and revealed by the Buddha and his disciples;

e. Any point or form of the Buddha-*dhamma,* or words in which it is expressed; and

f. Righteousness, justice.

It is in the last sense of the word, righteousness, justice that we are interested at present. The entire Buddhist ethics can be branded as *dhamma* or righteousness. It involves right thinking, right speech, right actions, and so on. One who acts according to *dhamma* or righteousness is called *dhammajīvin.* According to the *Dhammapada*: "People hold dear that man who is endowed with *sīla* and established on *dhamma,* and who knows the truth and minds his own business."[82] Thus *sīla* or morality is nothing but righteousness. Just as a monk is required to follow the *dhamma,* the householder must accumulate riches only with justice and fairness. He must not indulge in violence for the sake of riches. He makes himself comfortable and contented with those riches. He divides his riches and accumulates merits. He enjoys riches without clinging to them. There lies his righteous character.

Similarly, an ideal king is one who is righteous in his deeds and character. He rules over his people with justice and equity. He establishes himself not by scourge or violence, but by righteousness.[83] Thus righteousness is one essential qualification for both the rulers and the ruled. Another important element of righteousness is requital or recompense according to one's deeds or merits or demerits. This is clearly indicated in the Buddhist theory of causation. The doctrine that we reap as we sow is perfectly in accordance with the Buddhist theory of retribution and causation. While performing an action which is morally good or bad, we ought

82. *Dhammapada,* p. 217.

83. *Dīgha-Nikāya* III, p. 142.

to bear in mind that we have to meet with the results of it sometimes and somewhere, whether willing or unwilling. Thus righteousness becomes part and parcel of the Buddhist ethics. It is ideally represented in the very personality of the Buddha. He is the lord of righteousness.

As a system of self-perfection, Buddhism proposed the autonomy of ethical doctrines. But the moral precepts advanced by Buddhism are not merely ideals to be reified. They are the ideals to be translated into concrete realities. The idealism of the Buddhist ethics would be discussed in the next chapter.

4

Idealist Nature of Buddhist Ethics

IDEALISM is normally defined in two different senses. In one sense, the term "idealism" refers to practising certain ideals set forth by any philosophy, and in another sense it refers to an ontological position which holds that ideas are primary and the matter is secondary or derivative. Such a position is often contrasted with materialism. Here the ethical idealism of Buddhism is analysed in terms of a doctrine which sets forth certain ideals to be emulated by the individuals. The genuine ideals are those that are worthy of emulation. Mere reification of ideals does not bring about any individual or social good. The ideals are so called because they can be translated into concrete realities, for they are highly realistic and pragmatic. The entire Buddhist ethics can be treated as a form of idealism in this sense of the term for it always advanced such ideals that are highly realistic and practical in nature. Let us examine them in detail.

Evolution of the Buddhist Ethics

The ethical doctrines of Buddhism have some social foundations and implications. Human individuals are part and parcel of any organised society. In isolation from society an individual loses his identity as a human individual. Of course, it may be true that the Buddha attained Enlightenment under the *bodhi* tree as a result of intense austerities and deep contemplation. But he lived and flourished in a society whose conscious and unconscious influences were cast on his personality and thought. Every great saint represents the explicit flowering of the dominant forces of his time. The insistent and compulsive urgency with which the problem of pain and suffering represented itself to the sensitive mind of the Buddha was a consequence of the social ethos and spirit of that age in which he lived. The society of his time was pulsating with pessimism and monasticism and there were many wandering preachers. The Buddha himself was conscious of his moral teachings and their impact on the society. In the *Dhammapada* it is mentioned: "A supernatural person (a Buddha) is not easily found, he is not born everywhere. Wherever such a sage is born, that race prospers."[1] In the process of acquiring an institutional framework, ethical teachings demonstrate more social influence. Although the teachings of the Buddha are more oriented towards the emancipation of the humankind from misery and suffering, they exerted profound social influence.

A sociological study of the early Buddhist ethics receives added justification today when responsible leaders of people and nations are saying that the Buddhist ethical concepts of *avaira* and *maitrī* alone can save humanity from the brink of social disasters. Mahatma Gandhi's political success in modern India is an additional testimony to the view that the Buddhist ethics of *ahiṁsā* can have both social and political implications. The freedom movement of Gandhi was a vindication of the practical applicability of the Buddhist notion of non-violence on a national political scale. The sociological foundations of the Buddhist ethics significantly show its impact on common masses. A sociological study of the early Buddhist ethics not only reveals its sociological origins, but also its social implications for future societies.

If Buddhist ethics stressed on the development of moral

1. *Dhammapada* XIV, p. 193.

rectitude, and uprightness for the growth of meditative self-concentration and contemplative insight, yet it has social respect in the sense that the Buddhist *bhikkhu/bhikṣu* has to lead his austere life in the *saṁgha*. He is not isolated from the community. Even if he could, for some time, live in a cave or on a mountain or in a forest, he had to come into contact with the people for his food and some other needs for the sustenance of his body. Thus a monk is not alienated from society. The *saṁgha* is a type of religious community wherein one sees the deep bonds of a primary group. The *Theragāthā* refers to the ethics of brotherliness in the *saṁgha*. It is held that: "behold the company who learn of him in happy concord of fraternity. . . . The Noblest homage this to Buddhist paid."[2] The *saṁgha* provided an institutional basis for ethical life of the Buddhist monks. It also generated an atmosphere of direct and indirect suggestion of the primacy of ethical values. The individuals who desired to lead a moral life thus received reinforcement and intensification because of the existence of social fraternity. The individual monk is a cell in the organic confraternity of the *saṁgha*. The teachers and saints who advanced in the moral and meditative path (the *arhat*, the *anāgāmī*, and the *sakṛdagāmī*) were the loci of the sympathetic radiation. They always encouraged the initiates (*sāmaṇas*) in the path of the redemption of sins and sorrows of the world. The senior revered monks had attached to them the prestige and social status because of their wisdom and holy living.

The great religions of the world attributed super-human qualities to their founders, prophets, and their ethical conceptions. The religious leader is regarded as only the medium through which the divine being reveals the moral and sacred path. This tendency to attribute a super human origin to their teachings and conceptions is an aspect of the dominant trend of world religions to obtain adherence and

2. *Theragāthā*.

following by claiming a super-social source for their theological and ethical doctrines. But, there is no explicit recognition of any divine agency in Buddhism. Nevertheless, the Buddhists believe that the great truths dawned on the Buddha in a super-intellectual stage of deep absorption. Hence Buddhism in spite of its non-acceptance of a theistic agency attributes intuitional origin to its ethical doctrines. However, there are evidences to show that non-intuitional sources have contributed to the growth of the Buddhist ethical ideas. Some early Buddhists believed that if one had developed this sentiment of universal all-comprehensive compassion (*maitrī*), then one could obtain the capacity to tame not only robbers and enemies, but even wild animals. The Buddha was able to subdue the furious elephant Nalagiri by the force of compassion. The Jātaka stories depict the early lives of the Buddha, prior to the attainment of the Buddhahood, and state that the *bodhisat* used to live in perfect amity with even furious animals. This is another illustration of the operative force of compassion. From the sociological point of view, it is a corroboration of a magical potency of ethical virtues. In the Buddhist literature we find innumerable instances referring to the acquisition of supra-normal powers of the Buddha consequent upon the dawn of Enlightenment.

Besides revelation and magic, there is a third source for the growth of moral ideas, and that is pragmatic consideration for social adjustment and welfare. Every individual has in him the egoistic propensity to self-preservation. But this egoistic-self-preservation present in all individuals can lead to a regime of anarchy and chaos, if there are no rules of adjustment to settle social conflicts. Hence in the process of social accommodation, adaptation and adjustment, there is the evolution of socio-ethical rules. The concept of *ahiṁsā* must have evolved as a remedy to overcome individual tensions and struggles. In the later processes of intellectual refinement, these socio-moral rules of adjustment and management of conflicts and tensions are given an idealist appearance. This idealistic colour is essential to instil in people a sense of attachment and an obligation to obey the moral rules.

Social penalisation and external constraint are also employed to maintain these idealistically coloured moral rules to the extent that adherence to them is regarded essential for social cohesion and harmony. *Asteya* or non-stealing is a great moral notion, but since its maintenance is vitally essential for social preservation, the agency of constraint and institutionalised coercion is taken recourse to for its application. Thus it is possible to realise that the problems of social adjustment have also contributed to the evolution of the Buddhist ethics.

It has to be kept in mind that the desire for social cohesion alone does not explain the total meaning and significance of ethics. The psychological growth of a human individual also results in a chastening of his emotions. Thus we find the development of what Westermarck calls "moral emotions." According to him, moral disapproval is a way of expressing individual resentment against a specific way of action and moral approval. It is a form of retributive, sympathetic and altruistic emotion. The psychological growth of man leading to the emergence of flowering of moral emotions is not something mechanical. It is highly subjective. In the same society or even in the same family there may be persons of the most diverse temperaments. Early Buddhism accepts the concepts of *kamma/karma* and *saṁsāra*. Both these concepts have psychological foundations. The ethical orientation of men and their capacity to progress in the path of moral endeavours are determined by their past emotional heritage. Even the Buddha himself had to practise penance and austerities in several previous lives before he could attain the cognitive, volitional and emotional maturity and egoistic non-affectivity which the Buddhahood typifies. Thus we find that in the emotional evolution and development of the Buddhist ethics, the following four factors have to be stressed. They are: intuition, magic, social adjustment and moral emotions.

The ethics of Buddhism preaches the middle path between the extreme form of hedonism and utter and absolute self-abnegation and asceticism. This *madhyama pratipāda* or middle path is categorised as the eightfold moral way — the *ariya-aṭṭāṅgika-magga/ārya-aṣṭāṅga-mārga.* Although the Buddhist ethics avoids the extreme concepts of chastisement and penalisation of the body associated with the teachings of the Jains, the monkish ethics of Buddhism is definitely and pronouncedly ascetic and rigorous when compared to any utilitarian and eudemonistic standpoint. However, the Buddha showed the great courage of spirit in denouncing the grosser and harsher forms of asceticism. The Buddha held that he had propounded a moral way that is noble, and oriented towards the realisation of the Supreme Enlightenment. As indicated in the first chapter, there are eight great concepts in his moral doctrine. They are: right opinions (*sammādiṭṭhi*), right aspirations or volition (*sammāsamkappa*), right speech (*sammāvācā*), right actions (*sammākamanta*), right means of livelihood (*sammājīva*), right efforts (*sammāvāyāma*), right mindfulness (*sammāsati*), and right contemplation (*sammāsamādhi*).

Right Opinions (Sammādiṭṭhi/Samyakdṛṣṭi)

The Buddhist ethics cautions individuals not to entertain wrong opinions about the self and the world. There is no substantial or permanent self. Everything is made up of *dhammas/dharmas* which are under constant flux. The empirical world itself is an impermanent phenomenon. We must know this truth. Without realising the impermanent nature of the world we attach so much importance to the world and the objects of the world. This causes suffering when we are deprived of certain objects in this world. Also, we must possess the right opinion about the Four Noble Truths. It is the knowledge of these truths alone that leads us to *nibbāna/ nirvāṇa.* Our opinions about the natural and social world are the causes of our actions. False opinions lead to wrong actions and the right opinions to legitimate ones. The consequences of our actions are determined by the kind of actions that we perform, and the actions performed by us are the direct result of our opinions.

Right Aspirations (Sammāsamkappa/Samyaksaṅkalpa)

Right aspirations are needed for the growth of renunciation, benevolence, and kindness towards all living beings. The stress on right aspirations and volitions indicates the inwardness of morality in Buddhism. The *Dhammapada* holds:

> All that we is the result of what we have thought: it is founded on our thought. If a man speaks or acts with an evil thought, pain follows him, as the wheel follows the foot of the ox that draws the carriage. If a man speaks or acts with a pure thought, happiness follows him, like a shadow that never leaves him.[3]

The emphasis on right aspirations is an important advance in the direction of ethical intuitionism. It is an attempt to find the roots of morality in the chastened conscience of man. As Socrates and Plato preached against the external conventionalism of Cephalus and Polemarchus and the operational pragmatism of Glaucon, so also in the place of the traditional ritualism of the brāhmaṇas and the formal asceticism of the wandering teachers, the Buddha advocated and heralded the application of inner reason and volition to moral life. He taught the ennoblement and purification of human intentions. The concept of right aspirations has

3. *Dhammapada* 1 and 2.

tremendous social significance too. Modern psychologists are trying to examine the emotional foundations of tribal, social, and national conflicts. If our aspirations are good, not only can social tensions and international conflicts be resolved, but also can we build a better and happier world. It is true that in the framework of the Buddhist ethics, right aspirations are oriented towards the cultivation of the state of *nibbāna/ nirvāṇa,* but their social import cannot be ignored.

Right Speech (Sammāvācā/Samyakvāk)

Right speech is cultivated from abstaining from lying, calumniation, abuse, and fruitless conversation. An aspirant must abstain from back-biting and using foul language. A good deal of social conflicts is generated by the absence of restraint over the use of language. The avoidance of foul language promotes inner peace. As a virtue it also gives social esteem and prestige. The success of the Buddha, Christ and Mahatma Gandhi is partly a consequence of their modest and pacifying language. Offensive speech is always dangerous for the well-being of an individual as well as for society. Pacifying language produces perlocutionary speech acts which have tremendous psychological impact on the listeners.

Right Actions (Samakamanta/Samyakkarmānta)

The Buddha laid great emphasis on right deeds. Right actions lead to the formation of virtuous character. The Buddha repudiated the concept of a substantial soul or self, but he was committed to the conception of the causal operative character of the acts performed by an individual. It is mentioned in the *Dhammapada*: "To say one (person) acts, another reaps the fruits of those acts is not true."[4] Although there is no concept of soul as an unchanging spiritual being, nevertheless, we find in Buddhism the concept of the

4. *Dhammapada*, pp. 246-47.

continuity of character and personality. It may sound paradoxical. According to Buddhism, it is essential to perform right deeds because they lead to the formation of the right type of character. Right actions involve abstention from destruction of life. To quote from the *Dhammapada*: "He who destroys life, who speaks untruth, who in this world takes what is not given to him . . . even in this world digs up his own root."[5] In Buddhism we find the distinction between good actions and bad ones. The former are characterised by the absence of covetousness, jealousy and delusion (*alobha*, *adveṣa* and *amoha*). Right actions can be performed by one who conquered the lower passions. In other words, he is free from desires and illusions of the ego. Egoism is the cardinal evil because it generates false attachments and perversities. Good actions have two natural consequences. First of all they lead an individual to the realisation of the supreme goal of final extinction of all pain, evil, and sorrow. Secondly, they promote the collective welfare of human beings in society. It is true that in early Buddhism physiological and psychological aspects of actions have been emphasised because it is a religion of redemption, yet the social purport of good actions is not completely ignored. If good deeds are performed, then social adaptation and harmonious functional adjustments are bound to result. But the concrete performance of good works is a very difficult enterprise because it rests on diverse factors. Modern science emphasises the notion of heredity, which has a significant role to play in the development of character and personality of the individual. But, according to the Buddhist theory, parents and the family background of the individual, and social environment are also equally determining factors for the actions performed by an individual. Of course, we cannot rule out exceptions. A second significant force for the concrete eventuation of good

5. *Dhammapada*, p. 147.

work is the compulsive mechanism and demand of the physiological and psychological structure of man. There are some actions whose performance is impelled by man's physiological and psychological structure. This structure is built up on the accumulated heritage and impressions of the actions of past lives. It leads to the generation of *samkhāras*/ *saṁskāras* which constitute the uniqueness of individual human nature.

The supreme quest for any Buddhist is the attainment of *nibbāna/nirvāṇa.* But this perfectionist quest, in order to get internalised in human psyche and to be operative as a force of purposive propulsion towards the acceptance of the Buddhist way, had to be socially expressed. Ideas do not have a ghost-like existence in space and time. Before ideas can become operative forces they need some form of social habitation in the minds of men.

Right Livelihood (Sammājīva/Samyakājīva)

It has pronouncedly a social orientation. We come across in the *Dhammapada* that:

> Life is easy to live for a man who is without shame, a crow hero, a mischief-maker, an insulting, bold and wretched fellow. But life is hard to live for a modest man, who always looks for what is pure, who is disinterested, quiet, spotless, and intelligent.[6]

The virtue of right livelihood excludes many kinds of mean and vulgar activities. It can have diverse social implications. We can earn money through bad means, but such earning would not be worthy of human dignity. Aristotle condemned large-scale trade, monopolies, and use of money as capital. He called them unnatural activities as distinguished from natural finance which is to foster moral living. The Buddhist

6. *Dhammapada*, XVIII, pp. 244-45.

notion of right livelihood also implies condemnation of these acquisitive economic operations. There must be proper balance between profit and service motives of any trade. One should not pursue trade only to amass wealth by cheating people. This is precisely what is done by the capitalist countries. The societies have been converted into consumer-oriented ones. There is no service motive. On the contrary, the economic ethics of Buddhism is opposed to the individualistic notions of the self-interest of man and the maximisation of returns as morally valid criteria of economic action. The Buddhist ethics refuses to consider the realm of business as a separate compartment of life. It is part of the social life of individuals. Professional ethics is only an offshoot of social ethics. According to Buddhism, life is one integral whole and ethical norms seeking to control deviance and evil have universal say. The Buddhist ethical way conceives right living as a preparation for right concentration and meditation. Therefore, economic activities have only instrumental reality. They are only means, but not ends in themselves.

In the ethical philosophy of Buddhism, economics does not assume much importance. Economic action is a means and it has to be moralised in order that it may not impede the attainment of *nibbāna/nirvāṇa.* The idea of the moralisation of the economic activities is brought out in the following passage: "Those who in this world are wicked, and such as do not pay their debts, are slanderers, false in their dealings, counterfeiters, those who in this world being the lowest of men commit sin."[7] Although the eightfold path of Buddhism insists on *sammājīva* as a norm for an ascetic seeking the goal of emancipation, yet it is possible to extend the sphere of its operation. The right living involves giving alms, living

---

7. *Aṅgandhasutta* in *Suttanipāta*, p. 245.

religiously, protecting relatives, blameless deeds and so on. Similarly, right efforts imply a systematic psychological training. They imply the suppression of the rising of evil states and the eradication of those evil states that have already arisen. They also include the stimulation of good states and the perfection of those which have come into being. *Sammāvāyāma* is only a psychological and moral scheme of training and it has nothing to do with the Platonic and Aristotelian notions of gymnastics.

Right Efforts (Sammāvāyāma/Samyakvyāyāma)

Without putting an effort nothing can be achieved. All of us must put an effort to resist evil thoughts and desires from occupying the centre of our consciousness. It includes self-control, negation of sensuality, not entertaining the bad thoughts, awakening good thoughts and concentrating one's mind on the welfare of the society. For instance, there are certain issues that concern all of us. Global warming and climate change is an issue to be tackled immediately to save our natural environment from the brink of disaster. All of us are concerned with the problem of global warming and climate change, but we do not have commitment to put an end to this natural disaster. A concerted effort is needed from all of us to mitigate the problem. We are aware of the fact that rapid industrialisation has led to this disaster. The dumping of industrial waste in the rivers and oceans and the letting out of industrial pollutants into the open air have caused enormous damage to the natural life and eco-systems. The need of the hour is to change our lifestyles. One cannot think of a miracle to happen to take care of this impending natural disaster. On the spiritual side the right efforts enable an individual to conquer all the desires. One has to overcome the desires by controlling one's mind. The control of mind is possible through right efforts.

Right Mindfulness (Sammāsati)

It indicates the constant mental presence of the dominant goals of existence. It is opposed to any inertia and lethargy with regard to the supreme quest for *nibbāna.* It implies a conquest of all kinds of false cravings and hankerings. It stresses a strenuous desire to overcome dejection. The aspirant has to train his body and mind in such a way that he will be ardent, self-possessed and mindful. It is mentioned in the *Dhammapada*: "The disciples of Gautama are always set on the Buddha, on the law, on the *saṁgha*, on their body (*kāyāgata sati*), in compassion and in meditation (*bhāvanā*)."[8] The operations of the death are inexorable. Therefore, it is essential that immediate efforts should be made to attain the supreme knowledge. "Death carries off a man who is gathering flower and whose mind is distracted, as a flood carries off a sleeping village."[9] It is essential to cultivate the path of earnestness leading to immortality, because thoughtlessness is the path of death. The Buddhist notion of *apramāda* has been differently interpreted. It is translated as "diligence," and "earnestness." It is an essential supplement to the notion of right mindfulness.

Right Contemplation (Sammāsamādhi)

It is the culmination of the ethical process. Morality, according to Buddhism, receives its consummation in the attainment of the serene concentration of the mind. *Sammāsamādhi* stresses on inward cognition and reflective abstraction. *Samādhi* is a state of mind consequent upon deep meditation and absorption. According to the Buddhist scheme, there are four meditations that lead to the attainment of perfect concentration. The first *dhyāna* results in the attainment of

8. *Dhammapada,* pp. 296-301.

9. Ibid., pp. 47-48.

gladness and joy. The second *dhyāna* leads to the attainment of elation and inner peace and silence. By the third *dhyāna*, a person is able to neutralise all his passions and false presuppositions and assumptions. The fourth *dhyāna* results in the attainment of perfect tranquillity and self-realisation. To quote a passage from the *Dhammapada*:

> The *bhikkhu* who acts with kindness, who is calm in the doctrine of the Buddha, will reach the quiet place (*nibbāna*), cessation of natural desires and happiness. O *bhikkhu*, empty this boat; if emptied, it will go quickly; having cut-off passion and hatred, thou wilt go to *nibbāna*. Meditate, O *bhikkhu*, and be not headless; Do not direct thy thought to what gives pleasure, that thou mayest not for thy headlessness have to swallow that iron ball (in hell), and thou mayest not cry out when burning, "this is pain." Without knowledge, there is no meditation; without meditation there is no knowledge; he who has knowledge and meditation is near into *nibbāna*.[10]

Samādhi as obtained by the four types of meditations is a state of deep absorption. It is the attainment of knowledge by identity with the great principles of truth. It goes beyond the conceptual cognition of thought. In a sense, it transcends the Kantian conception of the free will willing the free will, because it is a process of unitive absorption in which both cognition and volition attain mature perfection. It is true that this perfection of concentration is highly personal and subjective in character. But, even this self-contemplation has also a sociological side. The processes and techniques of contemplation result in the development of an integrated, steady and self-possessed personality. The early Buddhist writings always refer to the delight and radiance that are spread over the face of a true disciple of the Buddha. This kind of integrated personality is in itself a social gain. Modern social psychologists have made us aware of the dangerous

10. *Dhammapada*, pp. 368-72.

explosions and conflicts that are the natural consequences of our frustrations and psychoses. The schizophrenic or divided personality is a great social problem. Hence if a person is able to attain a sense of delight, calm and happiness, he not only realises a great personal goal, but also renders a great social service. His personality emits sparks of happiness and peace. Therefore, it is clear that the existence of such a personality has a great social value. To quote from the *Dhammapada*: "Whatever place a faithful, virtuous, celebrated . . . man chooses, to here he is respected. Good people shine from afar, like the smoke of mountains; bad people are not seen, like arrows shot by night."[11] By stressing the notions of morality and contemplative concentration, early Buddhism preached a deep sense of morality. It provided an ethical teaching that inculcates profound purity and holiness.

Pragmatic Purport of the Noble Eightfold Path (Ārya-aṣṭāṅga-mārga)

The *ārya-aṣṭāṅga-mārga* is a very important contribution to the evolution of ethical ideas. It removes the subject of ethics from the domain of supernaturalism and transcendentalism. It preaches a moral way in which the individual is required to conform to the path of ethics not out of fear of the external agency, but because of inner source and impulsion. Its efficacy lies in the purification of intentions. The Buddhist way is a comprehensive code and it preaches a path that leads to the integration of personality and the attainment of calm, peace and silence. Although the Buddhist ethics is not supernatural in its foundations, there is an element of the a priori in the Buddhist ethics. *Samādhi* and *nibbāna* are super-intellectual categories and we cannot obtain a rational analysis of them. They do involve at least an initial faith in their certainty before the aspirant can take up the path.

11. *Dhammapada* (miscellaneous), p. 15.

Although there is an element of the a priori in Buddhist ethics as it is oriented towards the individual perfection and the attainment of *nibbāna*, the eightfold ethical way is chiefly intended to promote the ongoing social progress and structure. The adherents of the concepts of right speech, right actions, and right means of livelihood introduce better community relations not only in the Buddhist *saṁgha*, but also in the greater society with which the *bhikkhu*s come into contact. The modern school of ethical sociology believes in the betterment of society and maximisation of satisfaction by the rational realisation of human interests. The Buddhist ethics advocates the realisation of social peace and communal harmony and fraternity by taking recourse to self-abnegation. There is Fichtean conception of the perfection of society or of social justice in early Buddhism. But the concept of right means of livelihood, if practised on a collective scale, can provide the basic value for solving the social and economic problems of underdeveloped and poor nations. Most of the modern industrial societies have brought havoc on societies by plundering the natural and social resources. In these societies a section of human beings is treated as mere means to satisfy the ends of another section. Therefore, the modern economists are advocating the principle of conservation. If an extended social application is made of the Buddhist notions of right action and right livelihood in the economic activity of any nation most of the social problems would be solved.

Sometimes the critics of the Buddhist ethics hold the view that the eightfold path advocated by the Buddhists is not all that dynamic for it is highly introspective and contemplative in nature. It may be true to some extent for the eightfold path culminates in the attainment of contemplation. But we must emphasise that its dynamic character lies in its insistence upon the cultivation of will, patience, courage and an earnest and immediate application of the moral path. It should be emphasised that the action-orientation of ethics is implicit in the very name *mārga*. The Buddhist ethics is not a matter of formal intellectual acceptance of some moral code laid down by the authoritative doctrines. It is highly pragmatic. It does not give any scope for passive faith and blind belief.

Ethical Categories as Ideals

Apart from the *ārya-aṣṭāṅga-mārga*, the early Buddhist scriptures refer to another classification of ethical categories (*brahma vihāra*). They are: *maitrī, karuṇā, mudita,* and *upekṣā.*[12] (They are also mentioned in the Patañjali *Yoga-Sūtra*. Most likely they are derived from a common source by Buddhism and Patañjali.) *Maitrī* or *metta* is one of the most important concepts of the Buddhist ethics. It comprehends both non-hatred and loving kindness. Hatred does not cease by hatred, but it can be overcome only by means of non-hatred. According to the Buddha, it is an eternal law. The Buddha told his disciples that victory breeds hatred for the conquered is unhappy. He who has given up both victory and defeat is contented and happy. But the absence of hatred, arrogance, and resentment is only one side of the picture. The wanderer who wants to attain emancipation must practise non-violence.

The Buddha made it clear that he who strikes or insults the other is not an anchorite. According to the *Dhammapada*, one who inflicts pain on innocent and harmless persons meets with one of these 10 states:

> He will have cruel suffering, loss, injury of the body, heavy affliction or loss of mind, of a misfortune coming from the king, or a fearful accusation, or loss of relations, or destruction of treasures, or lightning — fire will burn his houses, and when his body is destroyed the fool will go to the hell.[13]

---

12. *Samyutta-Nikāya*, pp. 115-16.

13. *Dhammapada* X, pp. 137-40.

The social consequences of non-hatred and non-resistance are obvious. The tremendous sociological orientation of Buddhist ethics is brought out by the immense moral and spiritual significance attached to the concept of *ahiṁsā*. It is the single way to attain fraternity and even identity with the entire realm of created beings. It is profoundly said in the *Sutta-Nipāta*: "even as a mother watcheth o'er her child, her only child, as long as life doth last, so let us, for all creatures, great or small develop such a boundless heart and mind. Ay, let us practise love for all the world, upward and downward, yonder, hence, uncramped from ill-will and enmity."[14]

The Buddhist believer is expected to be extremely solicitous for the well-being and happiness of all living beings. The stress on kindness and love seeks to emphasise the notion which is essential both for social well-being and *nibbāna*. In early Buddhist literature, the cultivation of kindness and love is sometimes associated with the acquisition of magical powers. Even dumb animals and furious beasts are caught by the dynamic spark of *maitrī* and become absolutely docile and tame. Thus the superior efficacy of love is clear. From the sociological point of view, *maitrī* is the concept of social accommodation and adjustment because it profoundly transforms the character of the wicked and the violent. In the Jātaka stories we find numerous instances that indicate the transmutation of the concept of *maitrī* into the dynamic principle of self-sacrifice to others. The Jātaka stories constantly reiterate the theme of self-sacrifice for the good of other beings. In the older ethical systems of the Veda and Upaniṣads and the law codes, kindness and sympathy were stressed, but Buddhism excels every other moral doctrine in this regard. From the sociological point of view *ahiṁsā* and *maitrī* are principles of rational harmony and universal love.

14. *Mettasutta* in *Suttanipāta*, pp. 148-49.

Maitrī is a creative force of social development and it can safely act as a deterrent and counterpoise to the dissimilar and disharmonious forces of social tensions, contradictions and struggles. *Ahiṁsā* and *maitrī* not only lead to the growth of internal harmony but they also result in the growth of spontaneous sympathy and a sense of dynamic identification with all living creatures in their suffering. Thus the cultivation of *ahiṁsā* and *maitrī* can generate a sense of inner fraternity. This is absolutely necessary for the healthy growth of any society.

Some Western critics have tried to distinguish the non-hatred and friendly sentiments inculcated in Buddhism from the stress on love in Christianity. According to Oldenberg, Buddhism emphasises not the emotion of a world-embracing love but the peaceful feeling of friendly harmony. In the reiterated emphasis on the cultivation of universal *maitrī*, Oldenberg finds that, "not the groundless enigmatic self-surrender of love, but rather intelligent reflection, the conviction that it is thus best for all and not least, the expectation that the natural law of retribution will allot to such conduct the richest reward."[15] Schweitzer also has drawn a distinction between the Buddhist negativism of *ahiṁsā* and the active love of Christianity. From the standpoint of social psychology, it is essential to distinguish between non-hatred and friendliness on the one side and positive love on the other. But two reservations have to be made. First, from the standpoint of social relations, the difference does not appear very substantial because even in the *Sutta-Nipāta*, *maitrī* has been illustrated by the boundless love of the mother for the child. Secondly, in the Jātaka stories we find numerous instances of the overflowing love of the Buddha for all living creatures. Nevertheless, it seems correct to maintain that the

15. H. Oldenberg, *Buddha*, London: 1882, p. 292.

supreme goal of the Buddha is the realisation of philosophic detachment and indifference, while Christianity has stressed love for all human beings because all are children of the same providential father. In the early Buddhist literature, the reconciling and harmonising power of *maitrī* has been illustrated by the story of the son who forgave the assassin of his father even when the former had the weapon ready in his hand to finish the wicked assassin.[16] This story is a supreme illustration of the transforming power of *maitrī* when it is sincerely accepted as right action. In fact, A.B. Keith is guilty of reading the Aristotelian concept of prudence (*phronesis*) into this greatly edifying tale. He holds: "The element of calculating prudence is ever present."[17] Prudence is a cardinal virtue in Aristotle's *Nicomachean Ethics,* but has no worthy place in the Buddhist ethics.

Besides *maitrī,* the four *brahma-vihāra*s stress on *karuṇā.* It signifies a feeling of universal sympathetic identity with all living creatures. The Indian mind has always regarded the Buddha as an embodiment of kind sympathy. *Mudita* or cheerfulness is also an ethical category. Loving kindness, universal compassion and cheerfulness have great social function and role. They are oriented towards the realisation of a sense of fraternal identity that goes beyond the Greek concept of intelligent co-operative interdependence in a community (*koinonia*). The life of the Buddha typifies for all time the radical eradication of all socially disorganising sentiments. The concepts of *maitrī* and *karuṇā* can alone strengthen the foundations of any political and social group. The concept of self-interest alone is inadequate. *Maitrī* and *karuṇā* are the foundations of universal solidarity. They replace the notions of reciprocity by the idea of universal compassion.

16. *Mahāvagga* X, p. 2.

17. A.B., Keith, *Buddhist Philosophy in India and Ceylon*, Oxford: Oxford University Press, 1923, p. 117.

The fourth category is *upekṣā*. It is more individualistic in its orientation. It stresses the development of utter non-attachment to the ills, pains, pleasures and tragedies of the world. *Upekṣā* is the characteristic of the man of vision, who refuses to be enchanted by the allurements of the evanescent world. The *Sutta-Nipāta* thus defines a calm *muni*:

> without desire for pleasant things and not given to conceit and being gentle, intelligent, not credulous, he is not displeased with anything. Not from love of gain does he learn, and he does not get angry on account of loss, and untroubled by desire he has no greed for sweet things. Equable (*upekṣā*), always thoughtful he does not think himself equal to others in the world, nor distinguished, nor low; for him there are no desires (*ussada*).[18]

Thus the attribute of the monk is the cultivation of supreme indifference and non-indulgence. It is clear that this indifference can be acquired only by prolonged concentration and mental austerities. The stress on indifference shows the ascetic other-worldly orientation of the Buddhist ethics.

In early Buddhism there were three concepts which comprehended the ethical quest and the philosophic achievement. They are: *śīla*, *samādhi*, and *prajñā*. *Śīla* is a comprehensive code of moral life. *Samādhi* is of deep moral training culminating in contemplation. This point has been already discussed elsewhere. Morality and contemplation result in the attainment of deep wisdom. These three concepts are integrally inter-connected. Wisdom is purified by uprightness and vice versa. Where there is uprightness, there is wisdom. Where there is wisdom, there is uprightness. Concentration is the intermediate category in the transition of ethical purification into the attachment of profound philosophical vision and wisdom. All these three categories ultimately lead to emancipation.

---

18. *Suttanipāta*.

The internal composition of *śīla* is that it has five elements within it. They are: non-violence, non-stealing, non-adultery, not to indulge in falsehood and non-drinking. The prohibition of violence is socially very significant. A monk abstains from killing and injuring any living creature. He lays down the stick; he lays down all the weapons. He is compassionate and tender hearted. In addition to these qualities the monk must also possess *śraddhā* or faith, *darśana* or philosophic insight, and *bhāvanā* or cultivation, and meditation. The practice of truth has a great part to play in the moralisation and harmonisation of social relations. A monk is one who unites people. He does not indulge in separating people. He enjoys concord and promotes it.

In the Buddhist literature we come across repeated reference to moral categories, although we do not find a system of ethics without them as it is normally understood by the philosophers. These categories have great social implications. Sometimes the ideal virtues are categorised as 10 in number. They are: charity, purification of conduct, patience, earnest endeavours, contemplation, intelligence, use of right means, resoluteness, strength, and knowledge.[19] We also find references to fear of committing sins (*ottapa*), to purity of conscience (*anavajja*) and to sympathy (*saṁgha*). Buddhism also lays great importance on gifts. *Dāna* is positive social action that is good for healthy development of any society. It is gift bestowed on those who are passionless, who do not hate, who are free from vanity and lust. In the interest of the right allocation of the economic resources of the society it is essential that the virtue of gift should be wisely exercised.

Saṁgha or sympathy is another important virtue. It includes charity and gifts, gentle and unassuming

---

19. T.W. Rhys Davids, "Amity" in *K.B. Pathak Commemoration Volume*.

conversation, kind acts and a dynamic sense of all-identification with the totality of living creatures. According to Buddhism, the moral way of living, culminating in philosophic wisdom, is higher than the attainment of heaven or the establishment of imperialism on the earth. Therefore, it is evident that in the Buddhist scheme of values, the economic, social, and political spheres are rated inferior to the moral and spiritual spheres.

Early Buddhism took special delight in the detailed classification of the sins and evils from which a person has to guard himself. Murder, stealing, and sexual impurity are the three sins of the body. Lying, slander, abuse and fruitless talks are the four sins of speech. Acquisitiveness, hatred and error are the three sins of the mind. These 10 transgressions, if refrained from, are bound to have an ennobling effect on the pattern of the social adjustment. Early Buddhism also condemned sensuality, the desire for rebirth, ignorance and metaphysical dialectics removed from the ethical path. There are five basic hindrances to ethical perfection. They are: appetitive sensuality (*kamachanda*), evil desires (*vyāpada*), sluggish activity and lethargic dullness (*thinamiddha*), nervous excitement (*udaccha*), and scepticism (*vichikitsa*). Sometimes we get references to the seven fetters or impediments to moral realisation. They are: lustful indulgence (*anumaya*), abhorrence (*paligha*), unfounded philosophical beliefs (*dosali*), scepticism (*vichikitsa*), vanity (*māna*), attachment to the prolongation of physical existence (*bhāva-rāga*), and ignorance (*avijjā*). At other places we find mention of the roots of evils (*asusala malani*). They are: lying, delusion, hatred, attachment, and lust. It is true that the orientation of these ethical categories is towards individual perfection. But it is fundamentally incorrect to conceive of individual perfection as totally removed from the mechanics and dynamics of the social structure. The ethical and spiritual purification of the individual does powerfully affect the feelings and sentiments of other human beings. There are numerous tales in Buddhist literature to illustrate the deep and profound transformation wrought in the lives of those who were once socially destructive like thieves, robbers, and criminals.

Critical Reflections

We have discussed the way in which the ethics of Buddhism operates in one's life and society. Now a critical evaluation of the ethical categories would help us in identifying the gray patches in the ethical doctrines of Buddhism. The ethics of Buddhism is comprehensive than the traditional Brāhmanical identification of ethics with duties relevant to professional calling. It goes beyond the conception of ethics as a code prescribed for various *varṇas*. Therefore, the content of virtuous conduct is extended to all human beings irrespective of their *varṇa*. It is mentioned in the *Dhammapada*: "Not to blame, not to strike, to live restrained under the law, to be moderate in eating, to sleep, and sit alone, and to dwell on the highest thoughts, this is the teaching of the awakened."[20] In Buddhism, ethics does not consist only in the performance of external action but it is imperatively laid down that intentions should be purified. Even when Buddhism accepts the traditional and conventional elements in ethics it teaches the incorporation of a moral element in them. Thus the abstractness and externality of action is suffused with the concreteness of pure sentiments.

Buddhist ethics is not founded upon the command of any divinely inspired primordial law-giver. Hence the sanction behind the moral imperatives of Buddhism is not the authentic revelation of the divine will by an angelic prophet. The Buddha was a great teacher, but never expressed any

20. *Dhammapada*, p. 185.

divine will. The Buddhist ethical code is not rooted in the pre-existent conceptual pattern of the divine mind. According to early Buddhism, the actions performed by an individual have a causal efficacy and the consequences of the acts performed are brought forth almost by an automatic inexorable vehemence. So long as evil actions do not begin to bring havoc upon the doer he relishes them. So long as meritorious deeds do not begin to shed glory the doer is not inclined to their performance. Early Buddhism taught the almost cosmic operation of the law of *kamma,* and it provides the categorical imperative of the ethical path. The belief in this law amounts to the visualisation of social reform and innovation not on an institutional pattern and organised planning but by effecting a transformation in human character. The central theme is to purify human motivation.

There is a definite strain of individualism in Buddhist ethics. The final goal of an individual human being is to attain emancipation from suffering. The realisation of *nibbāna* which is the complete extinction of all pain and misery is the ultimate destiny of man. *Nibbāna* can be attained by all individuals, provided the right type of means is employed. The Buddha himself had to make tremendous efforts involving prolonged therapeutics of will and intelligence for its attainment. There is no concept of predestination in Buddhist ethics. *Nibbāna* is not the monopoly of a selected or chosen group of people. It is capable of being realised by everyone. To this extent, Buddhism reacts against the aristocratic element involved in the theodicy of predestination. The *Kaṭhopaniṣad* states that the *Ātman* can be realised only by him whom it chooses. But Buddhism teaches individual responsibility for the attainment of salvation. The Buddha wanted his disciples to be a light unto themselves and to rely on themselves. To quote from the *Dhammapada*:

> Self is the lord of self. Who else could be the lord? With self well subdued, a man finds a lord such as few could find. The evil done by oneself, self-begotten, self-bred crushes the foolish as a diamond breaks a precious stone. By oneself evil is done, by oneself one suffers; by oneself evil is left undone, by oneself one is purified. Purity and impurity belong to oneself, no one can purify another.[21]

This type of vigorous stress on individual efforts generates a profound sense of optimism. Buddhism explains the sinful and irrational structure of the world in terms of the deeds committed by individuals. Thus it teaches the individuals not to supplicate some external agency but to rely on their own efforts. Thus it prepares the foundation of an ethic of healthy and robust individualism. The idea that the individual can make or not to make his destiny is one of the greatest contributions of Buddhism to social ethics. It is a great challenge to all pretensions to automatic and aristocratic monopoly of the final wisdom.

According to Buddhism, there are two dimensions of a moral act. The morality of action leads to the attainment of heaven. Perhaps the early Buddhism derived from the traditional Brāhmanism the belief in heaven and hell. The doer of evil actions suffers twice. He suffers in this world and also in the next. The Jātaka stories refer to eight great hells and 16 minor hells. Sometimes this figure is raised up to 100 and more. The *Dhammapada* would condemn a liar to hell. To quote from it: "The virtuous man delights in this world, and he delights in the next; he delights in both. He delights and rejoices, when he sees the purity of his own work."[22] Thus one incentive to moral action is the attainment of heaven. Sometimes a better status in future is regarded as the fruit of

---

21. *Dhammapada*, pp. 160, 165.
22. Ibid., p. 16.

good deeds performed on the earth. The final goal of the moral fact including both actions and intensions is the attainment of *nibbāna*. The overwhelming trend of Buddhism is to emphasise the supremacy of the moral norm even when it teaches the ultimateness of *nibbāna* and *prajñā*.

Buddhism teaches the vast significance of *samādhi* and *nibbāna* for every individual. *Samādhi* is a state of deep and intense concentration. When one is engaged in *samādhi*, not at intermittent intervals, but as a matter of frequent duration, then it involves the element of adjustment to super-normal world. This means that the more the transcendent aspects of ethics are emphasised, the more the elements of withdrawal and ascetic rejection of the world would become pronounced. There is no question of identification with the norms accepted in the society. Thus the final ethic of Buddhism is oriented towards the ascetic realisation of other-worldly goals. Although the lay ethical doctrines of Buddhism are based on accommodation and compromise with the world and although common ideas, common interests and customs and mutual sympathy are stressed for the common people, the final and dominant note is withdrawal from the duties, sanctions, and obligations of the social life. Therefore, all the elements of lay adjustment with and adaptation to the community are of secondary significance. "How is there laughter, how is there joy, as this world is always burning? This body is wasted, full of sickness, and frail; this heap of corruption breaks to pieces, life indeed ends in death."[23] Hence the supreme goal is renunciation of the dark state of the householder's life and to make efforts for that realisation that led to the extinction of all sorrows and whence there is no return again to this tragedy-stricken world.

The Buddhist emphasis on resolute endurance,

23. *Dhammapada*, pp. 146-47.

forbearance, beneficence, benevolence, and sympathy is noteworthy. It is true that ultimately all the ethical preparations are oriented towards the attainment of *nibbāna*, but his does not really amount to the total devaluation of the mundane values and temporal interests of the lay people as alleged by the critics. There is no condemnation of the norms and techniques and processes associated with the adjustments of family and social lives of the lay individuals. The Buddha never preached social chaos and disorganisation. It is true that in this scheme of values the life of the ascetic who had renounced the home life was rated far superior to the life of the householder. This does not in any way mean that the life of the householder is insignificant. The concept of family is equally important for the formation of any society. Therefore, one cannot do away with the stage of a householder. The Buddha recognised its importance.

Early Buddhism marks the tendency to accentuate the monastic trends that were visible towards the end of the Upaniṣadic age. By exalting the life of an ascetic in quest of emancipation, Buddhism tends to build-up a separate sphere of spiritual ethics removed from the profane cult of those who were still immersed in the pleasures of the world. This premium on asceticism and the supremacy of the moral virtues associated with the life of the *bhikkhu* creates a sense of psychological tension for the average believer. On one side there is a deep-seated desire of man to find a family and lead a comfortable existence. On the other side there is the teaching of the Buddhist ethics that preaches the evanescence of temporal goods and mundane values.[24] The constant emphasis on the inexorability of death leads at times to a sense of nihilistic despair and utter illusoriness in the minds of ordinary men. The natural quest for self-preservation is subjected to a series of devastating onslaughts by the hymns

24. Max Weber, *Essays in Sociology*, p. 323.

in praise of the conquest of the ego or *ahaṁkāra*. Therefore it is held by many that the final goal of the Buddhist ethics is, in spite of the occasional discussions on lay morality, to build-up a system of soteriology and emancipation. The stress is not on social adjustment and the realisation of rational common good as in the Greek ethics but on the development and cultivation of an attitude of philosophic quiet and indifference.

The dominant stress on other-worldly orientation in quest of the extinction of pain and sorrow leads to the neglect of the conception of social rationality as the criterion of good life. All action impelled by the calculation of self-interest is suspected in Buddhism. Desire, in anticipation of any experience of pleasurable feeling, is regarded as the root of evil and hence individual economic activity in quest of the maximisation of individual profit can never find any theoretical foundation in the economic ethics of Buddhism. It is true that most of the psychological and moral attributes which are highly praised in early Buddhism do have direct and indirect social implications, but the absence of the conception of the primacy of social good and its rational realisation leads to the absence of any theory of social and economic justice. In early Buddhism individual hardships and privations are explained in terms of individual action and there is no attempt at the institutional and sociological analysis of the foundations of social irrationalities and contradictions. There is no elaborate attempt in early Buddhism to apply critical ethical judgements to the state and society. Hence Buddhism did not prescribe any thorough programme of social reform.

Only individuals are conceived as capable of moral action. The Buddha never sponsored any programme of the incorporation of morality and rationality in the structure of the state. Early Buddhism has no belief in an ethical state to be realised in the future. The transcendentally oriented Buddhist ethics never regarded the political structure as the embodiment of freedom, nor the actualisation of the ethical substance. According to the Buddhist scheme, emancipation is to be attained not by performing something good that is socially conforming, but by righteous mendicancy, intuitive perception and contemplative insight. Socially conforming works can at best lead to the attainment of heaven and good birth in the future. Hence there can be no ultimate motive for any definite interest in secular ends and positive programmes of social amelioration and betterment. Instead of stressing on the performance of good works, *nibbāna* is oriented to rending asunder the wheels of *kamma.* This transcendental stress implies the disassociation from all direct mundane interests.

But the quest for *nibbāna* does not mean any anti-social egoistic hedonism. It is a mistake to view that transcendental ethics is anti-social. The quest for transcendental values is absolutely removed from being anti-social. The only charge from a sociological standpoint that can be levelled against a scheme of transcendental ethics is that it does not adequately stress on social good. It is true that a transcendentally oriented ethical system relegates the pursuit of secular values to a subordinate realm. But the realisation of *nibbāna* can never be consonant with the doing of any deed that can have socially devastating implications and consequences. The charge of egoistic hedonism is not correct because, after all, the goal of the extinction of suffering has to be attained by the individuals themselves. There can be no vicarious atonement and no realisation of truth by proxy. The individuals are the loci of all those works and austerities that lead to the realisation of truth and emancipation. But a person who has become enlightened can serve the fellow-seekers after truth in two ways. First, he can impart teachings to them. He can be of help in resolving their doubts and solving their problems. Secondly, he helps in setting standards of an exalted excellence of moral character. Hence the seer can become a centre of inspiration and he can radiate moral and spiritual vigour and strength.

Buddhist ethics has certainly set before itself a transcendental ideal. Social, political, and economic ethics have a subordinate place here. The supreme and final goal being the individual's redemption from sins, sorrows, and sufferings, it is often viewed that it neglected the mundane aspects of social life. The attainment of *nibbāna* is the supreme imperative. Although the teachings of the realisation of *nibbāna* are introspective, subjective, and deeply personal, yet the spiritual and ethical quest is regarded not in terms of quietistic passivity but in terms of a mighty conquering adventure. Such a spirit of adventure is worth pursuing according to the Buddhist ideals. It is mentioned in the *Dhammapada*: "Who shall overcome this earth, and the world of Yama and the world of gods? The disciple will overcome the earth, and the world of Yama, and the world of the gods."[25] The interpretation of the spiritual efforts towards emancipation in terms of conquest indicates the dynamic and powerful aspect of Buddhism and it should remove any association of weakness or sluggishness with the ethical and spiritual life.[26]

Buddhism has set before us an exalted code of moral living. It certainly is a rigorous code but there can be denial of or doubt about its elevated tone and nature. The Buddha's unblemished life is one of the greatest events in the ethical advance of humanity. Buddhism has rendered a signal service to humanity by preaching the moralisation of human conduct

---

25. *Dhammapada*, verses 44 & 45.

26. P. Edgerton, "The Upanisads: What do they Seek and Why?" in *The Journal of American Oriental Society*, 1929, pp. 97-121.

and by stressing on universal nobility, compassion, benevolence and sympathy. It may not be possible to imitate the life of the Buddha for an ordinary man but the ideal that he has set can be worthy of emulation. Society would certainly benefit if these ideals and especially the concepts of non-hatred and loving kindness are incorporated not only in any culture but in the world culture as a whole. The pure, serene, and elevated life of the Buddha is a challenge to our lives engrossed in petty satisfactions and is a light for solving the neurotic discontents and crisis of civilisation. The works of the Buddhist evangelisation in the Far Eastern countries is a living testimony to the immense dynamic energy released by the powerful moral personality of the Buddha.

The above analysis exposes both the merits and demerits of Buddhist ethics. However, there are more merits and less demerits. No system is free from comments and criticisms. In the next chapter an attempt is made to show the relevance of Buddhist ethics to the contemporary social problems.

5

Buddhist Ethics and Contemporary Society

OUR project on the Buddhist ethics would remain incomplete if we do not show its relevance to contemporary society. Contemporary society can best be illustrated as a technological society in which every human individual is reduced to the level of a consumer. The survival of technological society is completely dependent upon the modern science which reduces every aspect of human life to scientific realism (scientism). Consequently, moral rationality (ethics) has taken a backseat in such societies. The erosion in moral values has virtually driven human individuals to a completely different kind of lifestyle that suits technological society. The individuals living in technological societies fail to realise the meaning and purpose of human life. Consequently they are unable to distinguish between what ought to be the case and what is the case. The former is concerned with the genuine needs of human individuals and has an altruistic motive. The latter is concerned with the false needs of human individuals which are imposed on them for the very survival of science and technology. Thus science is no more a social enterprise or an embodiment of human dignity. It virtually controls our lifestyle. The domination of scientific rationality over moral rationality has given rise to social problems that are peculiar to technological societies. They are the problems concerning climate change, human rights, euthanasia, abortion, homosexuality and so on. All these social evils are attributed to the lack of moral values. Morality has become a tool in the hands of science and technology. Axiology as a science of values comes to our rescue when morality loses its ground in a society where philosophical idealism (wisdom) is completely set aside due to the demands of scientific realism. Axiology as an important branch of moral philosophy reminds us of our duty as philosophers not to remain merely as lovers of wisdom but to act with wisdom in order to prevent social catastrophes. Under the sway of scientific realism modern man inculcates only those material values which are basically instrumental in promoting science and technology as the only legitimate mode of rationality. Such a view has dangerous consequences, for it fails to recognise the role of reason or rationality in any other field of inquiry. In this context it is interesting to observe the following statement of David Ingram:

> Today, many philosophers would argue that the rightness of moral choices and values cannot be rationally determined. If the moral decision is relegated to the sphere of arbitrary (private) preference, then only science and technology, logical and calculating thought, can lay claim to universal reason. But in a society in which the rightness of basic goals and values is assumed to be beyond rational assessment social practice itself — however, scientifically enlightened it may be — becomes irrational. When science and technology exclusively dominate social life they themselves become ideological.[1]

If rationality is the sole property of science and technology, then, as Ingram held, moral values remain as mere exhortations to certain virtues for they are arbitrary, private and emotional appeals of the speakers. The emotive theory of ethics propounded by the logical positivists like A.J. Ayer precisely holds this view. But it is not the case. Of course, the

1. David Ingram, *Critical Theory and Philosophy*, New York: Paragon House, 1990, p. XXVI.

fact (is) — value (ought) distinction is not new to philosophers and scientists. In his *Tractatus Logico-Philosophicus* Wittgenstein made the physical world as the domain of facts. And in this world there is no scope for values. If at all there are values they exist outside this world. But the later Wittgenstein realised this folly and brought them back to the realm of the physical world to show the co-existence of facts and values. This is a healthy sign, for otherwise there would be a perpetuation of Hobbes' state of nature in which there is a war of all against all. Moralists have often argued that values can neither be reduced to facts nor be derived from facts. This does not mean that rationality is confined to the realm of facts alone as if moralists are completely bereft of rationality while advocating a system of values. As regards the significance of values, one of the contemporary Indian philosophers Hiriyanna writes as follows:

> The place which values occupy in life is so important that no philosopher, whose theme is the whole of experience, can omit to take account of them.[2]

Broadly speaking, a value is something that is desirable. What is desirable is often contrasted with what is desired. The former has an altruistic appeal while the latter is pursued only to satisfy one's desired end. In other words, facts are apprehended, values are realised. These values are further divided into material and non-material ones. Material values are always weighed in terms of their immediate material value. A gold ornament has immediate material value. It can be exchanged for a sum of amount. More than its aesthetic appeal it is for its material worth people would like to possess it. By and large material values are only treated as instrumental values. They have mere extrinsic worth. On the contrary the non-material

2. M. Hiriyanna, *Indian Conception of Values*, Mysore: Kavyalaya Publishers, 1975, p. 1.

values such as ethical, religious, and aesthetic values are ends in themselves. They have intrinsic worth. When Socrates held that knowledge is virtue what he meant is that it is an end in itself. But there are always exceptions when people sell knowledge for material gains like Sophists and tell the truth, although they are congenital liars, for some material benefits. One can always find an exception to a rule.

Further it is asked: Do values belong to things, or do we endow things with value? As we know, the material value of a thing is not within the thing unlike the quality of hardness which is within the thing. This day-to-day example poses another question: Are values subjective or objective? There are moralists who treat them as subjective and there are also moralists who treat them as objective. Their arguments proceed in the following manner. The subjectivists argue that our experience tells us that values are relative for they differ from one social group to another and from one individual to another. What is viewed as an utmost value by one social group or individuals may not be so for another social group or an individual. What is sincerely admitted as desirable for one social group often turns out to be undesirable for another social group. On a cold night what is valuable for a person is the fire in the fireplace but not a diamond or a gold coin. Similarly the objectivists argue that values are not relative but they become relative to varying social groups and individuals. The reasons attributed to such a view is that values are consistent but they vary from one group or individual to another group or individual due to changing environment, circumstances, biological constitution and so on. Colours and beauty provide feast to our eyes, but it may not be so for a person who is blind or suffering from colour-blindness. We are unanimous in holding that a glass of milk is conducive for maintaining good health but not a glass of cocoa. If anything and everything is conducive for good health then we may value everything as good for maintaining good health. But it is not so.

To treat values as subjective or objective does not go well with them at all. It is unfair to values. A careful examination of values which we experience in our day-to-day life suggests that values are neither the exclusive property of objects or acts nor exclusively created by human beings. The values are both subjective and objective. They are subjective in so far as the process of evaluation is concerned and objective as the evaluation is always the evaluation of something objective or concrete. We evaluate standards of education, of life, of health and so on. The process of evaluation is the outcome of our reflective thinking. It is held by philosophers in general that reflection is the essence of rationality. Therefore it is meaningless to say that there is no involvement of rationality in moral evaluation. Rationality is not the prerogative of scientists. As rightly held by later Wittgenstein rationality assumes different forms in different forms of life. Similarly, both subjectivism and objectivism operate in all forms of life. Science cannot be an exception to this rule. One of the best criticisms of objectivism is found in Kant's *Critique of Pure Reason*. The pure percepts, which are supposed to be objective, without proper conceptualisation do not yield any knowledge. What is called conceptualisation is an inner process and its objective significance is only realised in the form of a judgement. Similarly, evaluation of any objective phenomenon is an inner process but its objective significance can be realised when it is experienced. All our efforts to reduce social life of the individuals to scientific laws would result in an unsuccessful endeavour, for "there is not yet much reason to expect that such a grand programme can be fulfilled."[3] Let us examine the issues like climate change, human rights,

3. Joan Robinson, *Freedom and Necessity*, Cambridge: George Allen & Unwin, 1999, p. 119.

suicide, euthanasia, surrogate motherhood, cloning, abortion, homosexuality, lesbianism in the light of the Buddhist ethics.

Climate Change

As aptly held by Ian Harris, one has to have a finer perception to identify the fundamental Buddhist equivalents such as "environment," "eco-system," "ecology," or "nature," which are of great concern to contemporary environmentalists. Therefore, the canonical, classical and modern epochs of the Buddhist history contain the *Tractatus Ecologico-Philosophicus*.[4] Climate change is a phenomenon which increases the average temperature of the Earth's near surface air and the temperature of oceans resulting in the disastrous consequences for life on the Earth. Climate change is a natural consequence of rapid developments in science and technology. Thus technological consciousness is dominating the modern age. All of us are concerned with the problems of environment as these problems affect everyone of us in one way or the other. Therefore, there is every need for a transition from technological consciousness to green or ecological consciousness in the wake of climate change. It is unfortunate that the Earth is gradually losing its capacity as a sustainer of life mostly due to man-made calamities such as deforestation, dumping of industrial waste in the seas and rivers, letting out industrial pollutants into open air, polluting the natural atmosphere with the smoke emitted by automobiles, etc. The modern lifestyle, which necessarily involves the use of refrigerators, air-conditioners, airplanes and so on, has caused enormous damage to the ozone layer resulting in the rise of mercury. In addition to that the life on the Earth is also frequently hit by the natural calamities such as tsunamis, volcanic eruptions, earthquakes, floods, gales,

---

4. Ian Harris, "Buddhism and Ecology" in Damien Keown (ed.), *Contemporary Buddhist Ethics*, London: Curzon, 2000, p. 113.

hurricanes and so on. It is also hinted by the environmentalists that the phenomenon called climate change may lead to a deluge for it slowly allows the glaciers to melt down. Therefore, the situation is going to be very serious and grave. The rapid developments in science and technology offer no satisfactory solution to the present-day ecological crisis and environmental degradation. They do not account for the meaning of life. The root cause of most of the problems is due to our blind adherence to a scientific world-view, which promotes technological (mechanistic) consciousness among us. It is a well-known fact that human rationality has both scientific and moral dimensions. The excessive emphasis on the scientific rationality at the cost of moral rationality makes science an ideology. Under the sway of science we tend to ignore the genuine needs of the humans sharing the resources of nature. Every living organism has its fundamental right to live. Human beings do not possess any exclusive right to live and disturb the natural habitat of other living organisms. The life on this globe is not a prerogative of humans alone. Not only that, since the natural life is not a human creation, humans do not possess any right to destroy it for their selfish needs. The technological consciousness, which is the backbone of scientific rationality, is no more an embodiment of the quality of life. In order to protect the quality of life on the Earth there must be a shift in our paradigm. In other words, we must look for a paradigm which offers a new world-view based on ecological consciousness (green consciousness). This new world-view brings about changes not only in the realm of science and technology, but also in our morality, and conceptual thinking. Thus it aims at a proper balance between scientific and moral dimensions of rationality.

Buddhism does not view humans as the only living and respected species on the Earth. Humans do not have any prerogative over other living creatures. Like other sentient beings on the Earth, humans also are caught up in the limited, conditioned web of *saṁsāra* or births and rebirths. What is interesting to note here is that of all births and rebirths, according to Buddhism, the birth and the rebirth of a human being is more precious, for it is only in human birth one can attain *nibbāna* or Enlightenment. In other words, the existence of humans is treated as a superior form of existence when compared to that of animals for humans have greater freedom and capacity to understand. Humans are responsible for technological revolution. Technology is their brainchild. But the unlimited use of technology is causing enormous damage to eco-systems and is solely responsible for environmental degradation. Man's unquenching thirst for material desires is the root cause of environmental degradation. The Faustian technology, which is the product of the West, is slowly spreading its tentacles. Consumerism has become the order of the day. Destruction of natural life is not acceptable to Buddhism, for the forests are recognised as ideal places for meditation for monks. It is held in the *Majjhima-Nikāya:* "These are the roots of the trees, these are empty places. Meditate, monks. . . ."[5] In fact, the Theravāda monks, who specialise in meditation, are called "forest monks." There is an evidence to show that the Buddha avoided any harm to a seed or a plant.[6]

Buddhism always advocated frugal living. It advocates the life of participation, but not the domination of humans on other forms of life. This symbiotic relationship between humans and other forms of life upholds the key Buddhist virtue of kindness (*mettā*). The practitioners of *mettā* do not harm any living creature deliberately. "There is no offence for a monk if he kills a living being unintentionally, not realising that his actions would harm a living being."[7]

5. *Majjhima-Nikāya* I, p. 118.
6. *Dīgha-Nikāya* 1, p. 5.
7. *Vinaya-Piṭaka* IV, p. 125.

However, one should not hold the view that Buddhism is against development or progress of human civilisation. Environment-friendly technology in the form of greenhouses, solar ovens, and hydraulic ramps is encouraged. The progress of civilisation in terms of material progress certainly brings about radical changes in the attitudes of humans towards nature, fellow human beings, and animals, plants and other forms of life. Every individual tends to use the other as a means to achieve his ends. This leads to greed and covetousness. Of course, material progress brings comforts of sorts, but one has to approach it with a balanced mind in order to uphold the Buddhist virtue, contentment. "Contentment is the greatest wealth."[8] Harmony with nature is the true Buddhist morality. In fact, "*Dharma*, the Buddhist word for truth and the teachings, is also the word for nature. This is because they are the same. Nature is the manifestation of truth and of the teachings. When we destroy nature we destroy truth and teachings.[9] In other words, forests are natural sanctuaries. Deforestation is a crime against life in general. It is an unpardonable crime. Progress and development should not be interpreted in terms of quantification, but in terms of quality. Faustian technology, which is the other name for modern technology, promotes false needs. "Quality of life cannot be secured without a purpose in life, and purpose in life cannot be secured unless we ascribe some meaning to the world, or at least some meaning to the human life — beyond the immediate gratification of our sensual desires."[10] The message of Buddhism to humankind is not to harm nature which is our natural abode. By destroying nature we are only setting fire

8. *Dhammapada*, 204.

9. M. Batchelor, K. Brown (eds.), *Buddhism and Ecology*, London and New York: Cassell, 1992, p. 99.

10. Henryk Skolmowski, *Dancing Shiva in the Ecological Age*, New Delhi: Clarion Books, 1991, p. 104.

to our own home. Therefore, one should not "live with a vocation that is harmful to humans and nature."[11]

Human Rights

Throughout the world human rights as a subject of endless debate in the legal, philosophical, social, and political circles has gained wider currency during the past two to three decades. In fact, the need for the concept of human rights arose out of the sense of insecurity confronted by human beings in their day-to-day life in different forms. The prevalence of sense of insecurity among human beings can largely be attributed to our Faustian attitude towards life in general. Faustian man hardly gives any importance to human values. Anything that arouses sensuous pleasure in him is desirable. Thus what is desirable is reduced to what is desired by a Faustian individual. This precarious situation faced by humans in the technological societies has ultimately led to the proclamation of the "Universal Declaration of Human Rights (UDHR)" on 10 December 1948 for the furtherance of human race on the Earth. The UDHR consists of 26 important articles concerning the nature of human rights. But, the UDHR to a large extent remained as a mere prescription rather than a binding force either on the state mechanism or on the individuals to protect the human rights. This is evident from the media reports how human rights are being violated either by the state mechanism or by the powerful individuals all over the world. Misuse of power over those who voice their views against the oppressive nature of the state, suppression of poor and weak, child labour, exploitation of women and so on have become the order of the day. One of the most important functions of a state is to protect the human rights. It must be impartial in protecting the legitimate rights of the individuals.

---

11. F. Eppsteiner (ed.), *The Path of Compassion: Writings on Socially Engaged Buddhism*, Berkeley: Parallax Press, 1988, p. 151.

Such a state alone is called a just state or welfare state. But in reality it is the state which uses its organised might against an individual or group of individuals for expressing dissenting voice against its policies. By and large a state represents the economically powerful section of society, for the former has to be dependent upon the latter for its political survival.

Now the question that arises is: What are human rights? Not only that, the language of rights necessarily presupposes the language of duties. If rights are privileges, then duties are obligations. In fact, the concept of right is predominantly a Western concept with a history of its own. According to Keown, there is as such no philosophy of human rights in Buddhism. He may be right in saying so.[12] In this context to quote Inada: "Admittedly, the concept of human rights is relatively new to Asians. From the beginning, it did not sit well with their basic cosmological outlook."[13] In Buddhism everything else is understood in the context of human nature. The manifestation of human nature prevails over other performative acts and individual rights. A similar view was expressed by Mahatma Gandhi when he was asked to express his views on human rights. He replied:

> I learnt from my illiterate but wise mother that all rights to be deserved and preserved come from duty well done. Thus, the very right to live accrues to us only when we do the citizenship of the world. From this one fundamental statement, perhaps it is easy enough to define the duties of man and woman and correlate every right to some corresponding duty to be first performed.[14]

---

12. Damien Keown, "Are there Human Rights in Buddhism?" in D.V. Keown, C.S. Prebish, W.R. Husted (eds.), *Buddhism and Human Rights*, London: Curzon Press, 1998, p. 15.

13. K. Inada, "A Buddhist Response to the Nature of Human Rights" in D.V. Keown, C.S. Prebish, W.R. Husted (eds.), *Buddhism and Human Rights*, p. 3.

14. M.K. Gandhi, UNESCO (ed.), *Human Rights: Comments and Interpretations — A Symposium*, London, UNESCO, 1950, p. 1.

Gandhi's view is not substantially different from that of Buddhism.

Human rights are those rights which ensure the dignity of human being by providing qualitatively better living conditions. They are elementary preconditions for an existence worthy of human dignity. In fact, they are the rights inherent in all human beings by virtue of their humanity alone in the sense that they cannot be purchased or granted. Such a view goes well with the Buddhist model, for the human rights form part and parcel of human nature. There are no human rights outside human nature. The Buddhist conception of human rights is based on the view that human beings primarily look for soft relationships with fellow human beings. Such a view helps us in understanding the fundamental nature of human rights. The Buddhist approach has many facets. The soft relationships with fellow human beings absorb anything that is hard. This is possible because the soft nature of the individual is characterised by openness, extensiveness, depth, flexibility, absorptiveness, freshness, and creativity. The soft nature of the individual cannot be overwhelmed by hard empirical conditions.[15] It is the characteristic feature of softness. It absorbs everything. This absorbing nature of softness is called *dhamma/dharma*. One of the Buddhist spiritual leaders of Thailand Buddhadāsa held that *dhamma* is the universal truth. It is the true nature of things. It appears to be void (*sunnatā/ śūnyatā*), but it is everything without referring to the self.[16] The *dhamma* represents openness and it encompasses everything. The problem of human rights arises only when we have limited ontological vision of the universe. The limited

15. K. Inada, "A Buddhist Response to the Nature of Human Rights" in D.V. Keown, C.S. Prebish, W.R. Husted (eds.), *Buddhism and Human Rights*, p. 6.

16. Donald K. Swearer, "Thai Buddhism: Two Responses to Modernity" in Bardwell L. Smith (ed.), *Contributions to Asian Studies*, vol. 4, Leiden: E.J. Brill, 1973, p. 80.

ontological vision is due to our attachment to empirical objects. But the unique coexistence of rights as privileges and duties as obligations or feelings is the saving truth of human existence, according to Buddhism. The first article of UDHR clearly states that: "All human beings are born free and equal in dignity and rights. They are endowed with reason and conscience and should act towards one another in a spirit of brotherhood."[17] Buddhism goes beyond this to hold that it is the true nature of *dhamma,* which is inherent in every individual, not only to act towards one another in a spirit of brotherhood, but also to exhibit compassion and kindness towards all living creatures. Therefore, its *dhamma* is not only restricted to human beings but also extended to the entire sphere of life.

Suicide

The social phenomenon called suicide can be characterised as self-murder or self-destruction. In his major and most influential work *Suicide,* the French sociologist Emile Durkheim writes that "the term suicide is applied to all cases of death resulting directly or indirectly from a positive or negative act of the victim himself, which he knows would produce this effect."[18] The purpose of Durkheim is to establish empiricism in sociology as against traditional interpretation of suicide in terms of psychological and individualist factors. The collective external forces have their own existence like cosmic forces. These forces drive an individual to this drastic act. Of course, Durkheim talks of types of suicide. It is not necessary to discuss all of them here. The impact of social forces on the individuals changes their individual and social behaviour. Whatever may be the case suicide amounts to killing oneself.

17. UDHR, Article 1.

18. Cf. Kenneth Thompson, *Emile Durkheim,* London: Tavistock Publications, 1982, p. 110.

This goes against the first precept of Buddhism. The Buddha said: "Whatever monk . . . should praise the beauty of death . . . he is not in communion."[19] Although Buddhism holds the view that there is suffering (*dukkha*) in the world, it does not advise the individual to give in to despair or loss of hope. If *dukkha* is prevalent in the world, it is encountered by one and all. One has to face it bravely. One's reflection on non-self (*anatta/anātman*) and on the principle of impermanence would certainly dissuade an individual from committing suicide.[20] If one treats it as a mechanism to escape from suffering, then one is abetting an act of cowardice.

People who have suicidal tendencies cannot face the unbearable life-situations. By annihilating one's material body one thinks that he/she is prepared to take up something less intolerable in the future birth. Although there is no direct textual reference to suicide, it can be interpreted that killing oneself is as good as killing another person. Therefore, suicide does not escape the injunction of the first precept. It is an unwholesome act for it is treated as serious as murder.[21] It appears that the Buddha ordered the excommunication of monks on two occasions. The first is when some monks killed themselves for their inability to understand the implications of a sermon of the Buddha on the "foulness of the body," for the body underneath the skin is so loathsome that it is not worthy of any attachment.[22] And in another case some bad monks persuaded a layperson to kill himself with a view to taking away his wife. They praise the beauty of death and

19. *Vinaya-Piṭaka* III, p. 73.

20. Peter Harvey, *An Introduction to Buddhist Ethics*, Cambridge: Cambridge University Press, 2000, p. 286.

21. G.H. Mullin, *Death and Dying: The Tibetan Tradition*, London: Arkana, 1987, p. 148.

22. Cf. R.E. Emmerick (tr.), *Suvarṇa-bhāsottama Sūtra*, London: Luzac & Co., 1970, pp. 320-22.

argue that a good person like him must kill himself so that he can have a good rebirth. This prompts the individual to eat rotten food to hasten his end.[23] Buddhism warns against inciting or aiding an individual to commit suicide. Also, it forbids any praise of death. There are many such passages in the Buddhist scriptures to show that suicide is a crime.

Euthanasia

Etymologically the expression "euthanasia" is derived from the Greek root *eu* (good) and *thanatos* (death), meaning good death or pleasant end. Unlike natural death, euthanasia involves conscious efforts by an individual to help someone to die happily. Is death a happy phenomenon? It is neither a happy nor an unhappy phenomenon. As rightly observed by early Wittgenstein: "Death is not an achievement in one's life."[24] An individual does not exist to share his achievement of death with others. Euthanasia is popularly known as mercy killing. It appears that Mahatma Gandhi, who is an embodiment of non-violence (*ahiṁsā*), asked his followers to put a suffering calf to mercy killing. He could not bare the suffering of the poor calf. It is a belief among many that euthanasia is administered to those whose life is not worth living. It is normally administered to terminally ill persons, patients with irreversible coma, and patients with unbearable suffering with no hope of recovery and so on. From the point of view of Buddhism, death is the most important and problematic existential crisis. Death is regarded as a transition from one life to another.

Sometimes the proposition, "It is better to die than to live" becomes a morally justifiable claim. This happens in the

23. *Vinaya-Piṭaka* III, pp. 72-73.

24. L. Wittgenstein, *Tractatus Logico-Philosophicus*, D.F. Pears, B.F. McGuinness (tr.), London: Routledge and Kegan Paul, 1961, §6.4311.

case of prolonged suffering leading to death. The onlookers of a person suffering from terminal disease often feel that it is better for him to attain early death rather than suffer like this. The acuteness of suffering drives one to opt for euthanasia. This is often called voluntary euthanasia. This does not amount to suicide for there is a greater appeal to reason in euthanasia and it is not performed by the person himself. In the case of suicide one decides to die not because he is terminally ill, but due to his inability to face the challenges in one's own life. The problems are more sociological in nature. The involuntary euthanasia is performed against the wishes of an individual. This, in a way, amounts to murder and it is an act of condemnation. The pre-voluntary euthanasia is a result of the decision of an individual who makes a living will by stating that in case he or she becomes physically or mentally incapable for the rest of the life under such and such medical conditions, he or she may be put to death. There is another case of euthanasia called non-voluntary euthanasia wherein a patient is incapable of deciding whether to die or not because the patient is in irreversible coma or suffering from Alzheimer's disease or an infant with abnormal brain disorder. In such cases there is a need to discuss under what criterion a person is declared dead.[25]

Voluntary and pre-voluntary cases of euthanasia are legitimate, according to Buddhism. It appears that it supported the ideals of the Hospice movement which is interested in assisting a person to have peaceful death. The Buddhist Hospice Trust was formed in 1986 to explore the Buddhist ideas concerning death, bereavement and dying and to develop a network of Buddhists who are willing to visit the dying and bereaved.[26] The Buddhist ideal is to die without

25. Peter Harvey, *An Introduction to Buddhist Ethics*, pp. 293-94.

26. Rev. L. de Silva, *Ministering to the Sick and the Terminally Ill*, Kandy: BPS, 1994.

any anxiety regarding those one leaves behind.[27] As Harvey puts it, "to die in a calm state, free of agitation, anger or denial, and joyfully recollecting the previous good deeds rather than regretting one's actions, means a good transition to future life."[28] In such cases of euthanasia the Buddhist monks are invited to chant calming chants along with friends and relatives to keep one's mind in a state of tranquillity.

But in the writings of Damien Keown one notices that there is sufficient evidence to show that killing in any form is not acceptable to Buddhism. According to Keown, one who follows the first precept of Buddhism "does not allow a living being to be killed, does not approve of the killing of a living being."[29] All the four cases of euthanasia are brought under the purview of killing. The reason attributed to this is that in the absence of permanent self the decision taken by an individual with regard to his own death is often changeable. Such a view is in conformity with the Buddhist theory of impermanence. Also, it is held that compassion being one of the Buddhist ideals there is nothing wrong in administering euthanasia for who suffers from intense pain and suffering. It can even be extended to animals. There is clear evidence in *Vinaya-Piṭaka* that it is not the case.[30] In all the cases of mercy killing the monks involved are held guilty of murder. It is also considered a defeat in the monastic life. The important distinction made between motive and intention by Keown is worth consideration in this context. Motive aims at the ultimate result of an action, and an intention aims at the immediate benefits of an action. But in any case life being the ultimate human value it cannot be subordinated to other

27. *Aṅguttara-Nikāya* III, 295-98.

28. Peter Harvey, *An Introduction to Buddhist Ethics*, p. 292.

29. *Dīgha-Nikāya* III, p. 48.

30. Damien Keown, *Buddhism and Bioethics*, London & New York: Macmillan, 1995, pp. 60-64, 171-73.

values such as friendship or compassion. Therefore, compassion as a motive leads to intention called killing or taking someone's life. This is totally unacceptable to Buddhism. But a Mahāyāna Buddhist may treat it in a different way. According to him the compassion killing is meant to safeguard others from the victim's evil deeds. In a way this is to stop bad *karma*. The Theravāda Buddhists, according to Ratanakul, do not carry out killing without the thought of ill-will or repugnance towards *dukkha*.[31] A doctor's motive of compassion in the case of mercy killing is admirable, but his aversion towards the patient's pain is also part of his motive. In the process, "subconsciously he transfers his aversion to the suffering to the one who embodies it."[32]

There are also cases of non-intended death. On Buddhist principles the genuine cases of euthanasia are unethical. But the cases that are mistakenly viewed as the cases of euthanasia are not unethical. For instance, the intention of the doctor who treats a patient is to cure his or her disease. However, there are occasions where the responses of the patients go contrary to the expectations of the doctors who treat them. If the patient's body can withstand the administering of a powerful drug, the dosage of the drug is gradually increased. There is a possibility that it reaches a toxic level. Consequently, the patient dies. This is purely an accident. It is not the intention of the doctor to kill the patient.[33] A monk suffering from a disease may be treated by other monks by giving some medicine. But the treatment results in the death of the monk. They are not held guilty, for it is not their intention to kill

---

31. P. Ratanakul, "Bioethics in Thailand: The Struggle for Buddhist Solutions", *Journal of Medicine and Philosophy*, 13, 1988, p. 310.
32. Ibid.
33. U.P. Hammerli, "A Definition from the Viewpoint of a Physician", in G.C. Oosthuizen, H. Shapiro and S.A. Strauss (eds.), *Euthanasia*, Cape Town: Oxford University Press, 1978, p. 192.

him. But if it were their intention to kill him, then it is a grave offence.[34] It is evident that for Buddhism life being very precious killing in any form is unacceptable. The Buddhist ideal is to help an individual to make best use of his/her present life in order to have respectable future rebirth.

Abortion

The premature termination of life during gestation is technically called abortion. But every case of termination of pregnancy cannot be characterised as an act of abortion. The natural and happy termination of pregnancy results in the birth of a live, healthy baby. An accidental or unintentional death of the foetus due to surgical operation cannot be treated as abortion. Only those acts that intentionally end pregnancy resulting in the loss of the foetus are called abortion. Spontaneous abortions and miscarriages cannot be brought under the cases of abortion. They are the physiological processes in the mother's body that destroy the foetus. The process of gestation starts with the conception of the female resulting in the formation of a zygote which develops into an embryo in about seven weeks. The embryo further develops into foetus until the fully grown child is delivered from the mother's womb.

It is mentioned in the *Dhammapada*: "Hard to gain is human rebirth."[35] Thus human life begins with conception and ends with the annihilation of the physical body. It is interesting to note here that for Buddhism life is a series of changing states. Life starts with the descent of consciousness into the embryo and passes through continuous changes. Thus it is not an emergent property of this process. The following passage is found in the Theravāda collection of *sutta*s: "Were

34. *Vinaya-Piṭaka* III, pp. 82-83.

35. *Dhammapada*, 182.

consciousness (*vinnanam/vijñānam*), Ānanda, not to fall into the mother's womb, would the sentient body (*nāma-rūpam*) be constituted there? "It would not, Lord." Were consciousness fallen into the mother's womb, to turn aside from it, would the sentient body come to birth in this present state? "It would not, Lord."[36] In other words, the consciousness of the past being enters the new being as a necessary condition for the development of life (body) in the womb. This is how the physical body is endowed with mental abilities such as sentience, volition, feeling, identification, sensory stimulation, and attention.[37] Of course, at present, we are not interested in the biological interpretation of how the processes of fertilisation and implantation take place. The Theravāda Buddhist view is that since there are no between-lives, the consciousness of an individual who just died is instantaneously transferred to a new life. The instantaneously transferred consciousness is called *gandhabba/gandharva* in the Theravāda literature. According to Harvey, "there is substantial body of evidence to support the idea of such a between-lives state, with the *gandhabba* as a kind of mutable, restless, "spirit" seeking out a new rebirth to "fall" into.[38] Damien Keown replaces the expression "descent" with the expression "enter" to substantiate the view that "we have every reason to locate the descent of the intermediate being at fertilisation."[39]

It is evident from the above analysis that for Buddhism life starts with the formation of embryo in mother's womb. Causing injury or death to life is an offence. The termination of life while it is in the womb is called abortion, and the termination of life after its immediate birth is called

36. *Dīgha-Nikāya* II, pp. 3-4.

37. *Samyutta-Nikāya* II, pp. 3-4.

38. Peter Harvey, *An Introduction to Buddhist Ethics*, pp. 312-13.

39. Damien Keown, *Buddhism and Bioethics*, p. 79.

infanticide. Both the acts are prohibited by Buddhism. The important passage from *Vinaya-Piṭaka* reads as follows:

> When a monk is ordained he should not intentionally deprive a living being of life, even if it is only an ant. Whatever monk deprives a human being of life even (*antamaso*) down to destroying an embryo (*gabba-pātanam-upādāya*), he becomes not a (true) renouncer, not a son of the Sākiyans.[40]

Similar is the case with Tibetan interpretation of *Vinaya* by the *Sarvāsthivādins*. As Harvey puts it, there is another important reason why Buddhism treats abortion a serious crime against humanity in general, for human life with all its potential for moral and spiritual development is so precious.[41] Both the perpetrators and the abettors of abortion are equally held guilty of the crime. According to Keown, causing deliberate death to foetus is as good as killing an adult.[42] In all, causing deliberate death or injury to human life is a highly punishable offence, according to Buddhism. Thus abortion is not an exception to this rule.

However, there are certain forms of abortion which are performed under specific circumstances when there is a threat to mother's physical or mental health, malformation of foetus which may lead to serious health problems. Also, it may be due to other socio-economic factors. Does Buddhism allow abortion in above-mentioned cases? Under extraordinary circumstances Buddhism allows it as a highly regrettable necessary evil. Even the classical Hindu texts forbid abortion, but for saving the life of the mother.[43]

40. *Vinaya-Piṭaka* I, p. 97.
41. Peter Harvey, *An Introduction to Buddhist Ethics*, p. 314.
42. Damien Keown, *Buddhism and Bioethics*, p. 93.
43. J.J. Lipner, "The Classical Hindu View on Abortion and the Moral Status of the Unborn" in H.G. Coward, J.J. Lipner, and K.K. Young (eds.), *Hindu Ethics: Purity, Abortion and Euthanasia*, Delhi: Sri Satguru Publications, 1991, p. 60.

According to Keown, it is possible even Buddhism adopts such a view.[44] How about contraception? In some Buddhist countries, especially in Thailand and Sri Lanka, to arrest population explosion this measure is taken by their respective governments.[45] Majority of the young women in Thailand who did not want children resorted to contraception. Even in Tibet, it appears, contraceptive methods are not opposed. The Lama Khenchen Thranggu Rimpoche happened to say "I see no great fault in preventing conception."[46] Since contraception does not destroy human life it is less objectionable. It is only a preventive method rather than a method to destroy life. However, the consequences resulting from the adoption of the method of contraception are as follows. First of all, it encourages illicit sex relationships. Secondly, it might result in the gradual decline in the Buddhist population. Thirdly, it prevents more beings attaining human rebirth. But these results may be less damaging or harmful when compared to abortion which directly leads to taking of human life.

Homosexuality

Homosexuality and lesbianism are two unusual practices of men and women in which men indulge in sex-relationships with men and women with women respectively. This unnatural and unhealthy practice is of great concern. The same sex relationship was admired as brotherly or filial affection. Sometimes it is also viewed as an affectionate respect to a spiritual master or a strong bond of friendship between

44. Damien Keown, *Buddhism and Bioethics*, p. 193.
45. T.O. Ling, "Buddhist Factors in Population Growth and Control: A Survey Based on Thailand and Ceylon", *Population Studies*, 23(1), 1969, pp. 53-60.
46. D. Stott, "Buddhadharma and Contemporary Ethics: Some Notes on the Attitude of Tibetan Buddhism to Abortion and Related Procedures", *Religion*, 1992, 22, p. 174.

two males or females. But this kind of relationship gradually turned out to be an erotic relationship where there is conscious identification of a person as a "homosexual," "gay" or "lesbian." This is the latest phenomenon and is on the increase all over the globe. According to Gilbert Herdt, there are at least three different types of homosexuality. In the age-structured homosexuality people of the same sex but of different ages involve in sexual activity. In gender-reversed homosexuality, a person tries to appear like a member of the fair sex by dressing and acting like a woman. And in role-specialised homosexuality a person is permitted to enter into homosexuality by virtue of his or her social and religious role.[47] All these forms of homosexuality are condemned by all societies in the past and even in present. Now the question before us is whether Buddhism allows these queer acts of humans.

It appears that natural sex-change is acknowledged by the Buddha. The early Buddhism accepted sex-change in a person within one life or between lives. There is a reference to this in the *Vinaya*, according to which a monk and a nun experienced a sex change in them. It appears that the Buddha accepted it as a natural phenomenon and addressed them as former monk and former nun in order to tell them to follow the rules of a nun and the rules of a monk respectively after the sex-change. The causes of sex changes, according to Buddhism, are kārmic in nature.[48] In the *Dhammapada* commentary there is a reference to a monk turning into a beautiful woman when he is attracted by another monk and marrying him to give birth to children, and again turning back to his original status as a monk and seeks forgiveness of the monk. This act does not deprive the monk, who turned

47. G. Herdt, "Homosexuality" in M. Eliad (ed.), *The Encyclopedia of Religion*, London: Callier Macmillan, 1987, vol. VI, p. 446.

48. Peter Harvey, *An Introduction to Buddhist Ethics*, p. 412.

as a beautiful woman, of the *arhatship*.[49] In other words mere sex change does not prevent anyone from being a spiritual person.

There is another class of individuals who possess the characteristics of both sexes. They are known as hermaphrodites (*ubhato-byañjanakā*). Since there is a possibility of a hermaphrodite seducing or enticing a monk or a nun in the monastery they are not ordained, according to Buddhism.[50] Buddhaghoṣa, the Theravāda commentator, claimed that there existed female hermaphrodites who both impregnated others and also got pregnant. And male hermaphrodites, who could not become pregnant, sexually attracted both males and females.[51] These characteristics are caused by the kārmic particles of one's past life. A person can overcome these characteristics through deep repentance and faith in the Buddha image. The great Buddhist text *Milindapañha* contains references to hermaphrodites and eunuchs (*pandakas*) along with other categories of individuals claiming that they cannot understand the essence of *dhamma*.

What is the status of eunuchs (*pandakas*)? According to Zwilling, a *pandaka* is one who does not possess testicles.[52] It appears there were no eunuchs during pre-Muslim era. A person is made into a eunuch by deliberate castration. It is rather used in a metaphorical way to address a person who has "no balls." But in *Vinaya* we come across-references to *pandakas*. The appellation is applied to a man who does not have male characteristics and also to a woman who does not possess female characteristics. This particular category is also

49. *Dhammapada Commentary*, I, pp. 325-32.
50. *Vinaya-Piṭaka* I, p. 89; II, p. 271.
51. *Aṭṭhasālinī*, pp. 322-23.
52. L. Zwilling, "Homosexuality as Seen in Indian Buddhist Texts", in J.I. Cabezon (ed.), *Buddhism, Sexuality and Gender*, New York: State University of New York Press, 1992, p. 204.

viewed as one that neither possesses male characteristics nor female ones. A *pandaka* is just an opposite of a hermaphrodite. Like hermaphrodites, *pandakas* are also debarred from ordination.[53] A *pandaka* is considered to be a passive homosexual who indulges in promiscuity by Buddhism. Therefore, a *pandaka* is not eligible for ordination.

Gender Equality

Nature has divided humans into men and women. Each group is endowed with certain natural characteristics. What is expected of men biologically is not expected of women and vice versa. It only shows that nature is impartial towards men and women. The feminists claim that gender is a social construction. But this construction is absolutely necessary for balancing our social environment. The general view is that women in general are deprived of many a right in the society. Like men, women must have equal access to religious teachings and practices. Equal status must be granted to women with regard to specialist religious roles. They must be granted equal rights with men in every aspect of social life. Discrimination of any sort is viewed as a discrimination against fair sex. The gender inequality, in almost all the cultures, affects only women but not men. Hierarchically men are placed above women. This is not accepted if natural justice is to be guaranteed. Of course, the expression "equality" has many connotations, and its meanings vary from one context to another. The common perceivable understanding of equality is that women, like men, should be granted equal access to the world shared by both sexes.

In classical Hinduism the duties of men are clearly demarcated from the duties of women for the purpose of greater harmony in families and societies. Their social roles are well defined. In Hinduism both male gods and female

53. *Vinaya-Piṭaka* I, pp. 85-86.

gods are worshipped and they have equal status in Hindu pantheon. This itself is an indication that men and women together constitute one single reality. The concept of *ardhanārī* clearly establishes this view. Any ritual performed by a man becomes incomplete without a woman.[54] The motto of performing a ritual is fulfilled only when wife and husband together performed that ritual. However, at the advent of modern era women felt neglected in ever so many ways. Also, it is true that what was originally intended by the Hindu Dharmaśāstras is sometimes deliberately misrepresented or misinterpreted for the benefit of a section of individuals. Women are not an exception to this bias. Partly, it is the changing perception of our social world and modern lifestyle, which is the result of Western culture, that gradually changed the equations between men and women. This resulted in feminist movements all over the globe to redefine the status of women in particular and gender in general. Men and women are two sides of the same coin. Both have equal role to play in the society or in any social organisation. The polarity between men and women only worsens the situation. Let us examine the Buddhist solution to this problem.

There is a clear indication in the Buddhist texts that women are never viewed as objects of sex or as mere child-bearers. It is always preferred to have a wise, virtuous, and courageous woman as daughter than a man as son. The Buddha never discriminated monks from nuns, and laymen from laywomen. All are eligible to practise *dhamma*.[55] The spiritual path is equally open to both. Sex and gender differences hardly matter for soteriological purposes. According to Hornrer, during the Buddhist era women "commanded more respect and rank as individuals. They

54. L.S. Dewaraja, *The Position of Women in Buddhism*, Kandy: BPS, 1981, pp. 6-7.

55. *Samyutta-Nikāya* I, pp. 196.

enjoyed more independence, and a wider liberty to guide and follow their own lives."[56] Another interesting feature is that the Buddha granted women *arhatship*. Just as monks can become *arhats*, so also nuns. Even celibate laywomen and laymen are eligible to become *arhats*. One comes across references in the *Therīgāthā*, the Pāli canon, that as many as 73 verses are devoted to 102 early nun *arhats*.[57] Even in Mahāyāna, Buddhahood is granted to all those women who perfect their wisdom (*prajñā-pāramitā*). Thus there is ample evidence to show that Buddhism granted equal status to men and women. The Theravāda Jātakas contain stories about virtuous and wise women.[58]

Trade and Economy

In the *Dhammapada* we find an interesting statement: "Hunger is the greatest illness. . . . Contentment is the greatest wealth."[59] Economy, trade and commerce are the backbone for the material progress of any country. The two main evils that always haunt human beings are hunger and poverty. If a country could take care of its citizens by not letting them be the victims of these two evils then that country is termed materially prosperous. In the Eightfold Path of Buddhism, "right livelihood" is emphasised. Every individual is expected to live happily and with contentment. Dishonest way of living just for the sake of earning beyond one's requirement causes suffering and is treated as unethical by Buddhism. The fundamental tenets of the Buddhist economic ethics are as follows. One must earn his wealth without violence and deceit. Such an earning is always praiseworthy. Anything earned by

---

56. I.B. Horner, *Women Under Primitive Buddhism: Laywomen and Almswomen*, London: Routledge & Kegan Paul, 1930, p. 82.
57. Peter Harvey, *An Introduction to Buddhist Ethics*, p. 358.
58. Jātaka with Commentary II, pp. 121-25.
59. *Dhammapada*, 203-4.

resorting to violence, cheating, and other unethical means is blameworthy. Whatever one earns must be spent for right purposes that promote peace and social harmony. Charity, compassion, and philanthropy would lead to karmically fruitful actions. Similarly, if one leads a miserly life even after possessing so much wealth and does not part with his earnings he accumulates bad *karma*. Lack of contentment even after accumulating so much wealth is blameworthy.

Dishonest livelihood may fetch immediate pleasure, but causes immense pain and suffering ultimately. Buddhism prohibits wrong livelihood which includes trade in arms and ammunition, animals meant for slaughter, mescals, alcohol, drugs, poison and so on.[60] Greed, stealing, lying for gain, and deception are seen as the avenues for wrong livelihood. A good tradesman takes care of his employees' needs and arranges for good working conditions and provides them water, food, and sufficient wages. Taking care of them when they are ill and letting them off the work at the right time are the good qualities of a tradesman.[61] Similarly, the workers must earn the faith on their employer and give him good support so that his business thrives. A moral and spiritual life free from laziness from either side improves the working conditions and leads to the prosperity of individuals and nation. One needs to be skilful and industrious in his work. Vigilance, caution, dwelling in an ideal place, balanced life, taking care of ones' positions, spending in proportion to one's earnings are treated as dhārmic way of life. Similarly, in the *Dhammapada* it is mentioned that there are six ways of losing one's wealth. They are addiction to drinks, drugs that produce sloth, haunting the streets, attending fairs, gambling, and cultivating bad company.[62] A good workman should not give

60. *Aṅguttara-Nikāya* III, p. 208.

61. *Dhammapada* III, 191.

62. Ibid., III, 182.

excuses for not doing his work unless the reasons are genuine. Another important thing is that one should not run into debts. Debt ruins one's peace of mind.

Buddhism does not treat wealth as an evil. But it has to be used for right purposes. It must be useful for oneself and also for others. Often the wealth ruins an individual. It puts him on a wrong track. An ideal person is one who remains calm even if he gains or loses in terms of his wealth. The middle path of the Buddha teaches us that one should not be too greedy to amass wealth beyond one's requirement and at the same time one should not remain in penury so that he or she is dependent on others for a living. It is the obligation of the king or ruler to ensure social and economic justice to all his subjects. There is always a great concern for modes of acquisition and distribution. Of course, one's poverty and wealth are attributed to one's past *karma*. Yet, as rightly held by Phra Rājavaramuni:

> A wealthy man can do much more either for the better or for the worse of the social good than a poor man . . . acquiring wealth is acceptable if, at the same time, it promotes the well-being of a community or society.[63]

Buddhist economic development is based on the Buddha's middle path. There is no need for highly technologically oriented production which may cause destruction to the natural life in many ways. Global warming is a direct outcome of high technological pursuits of Faustian man. We can very well satisfy our needs with intermediate technology which is eco-friendly and less destructive. Excessive use of technological apparatus ruins the rural economy. This leads to unemployment and exodus of villagers from their natural

63. Phra Rājavaramuni, "Foundations of Buddhist Social Ethics", in R.F. Sizemore, D.K. Swearer (eds.), *Ethics, Wealth, and Salvation: A Study in Buddhist Social Ethics*, Columbia (SC), University of South Carolina Press, 1990, p. 45.

habitat to semi-urban and urban civilisation.[64] The need of the hour is to protect our natural home from destruction. The only way to save it from technological destruction is to base our production and economy on the Buddhist model that recommends middle path.

Violence and Peace

The Hindu saints always held that violence breeds further violence. Buddhism welcomes such a view. In the *Dhammapada* it is mentioned: "Enmities never cease by enmity in this world; only by non-enmity do they cease. This is an ancient law."[65] The present age is marred by violence of sorts. Peace has become a rare commodity. Greed, hatred and delusion are the root cause of violence.[66] Desire is the root cause of greed. Greed leads to power and power leads to attachment to material objects, pleasures, property, position, territory, economic domination, and political superiority. In order to safeguard one's wealth a person tries to remain politically powerful. Our attachment to material world is due to ignorance. Sometimes violence erupts due to distorted perceptions of an issue, which is blown out of proportion, or due to the influence of other members of one's own community. Therefore, it is the responsibility of every individual to know the truth before indulging in any violence. It is also the tendency of many to provoke individuals by their actions and talk to resort to violence. The Buddha advised his disciples not to get provoked even if someone makes disparaging remarks against the Buddha, the *dhamma*, and the *saṁgha*.

Buddhism always insists that one has to conquer not only

64. E.F. Schumacher, *Small is Beautiful: A Study of Economics as if People Mattered*, London: Blond and Briggs, 1973, p. 56.

65. *Dhammapada*, 5.

66. Nyanaponika, *The Roots of Good and Evil*, Kandy: BPS, 1978, p. 50.

his passions and emotions but also one's anger. The following statements vindicate these points. "Conquer anger by love, conquer evil by good, conquer the stingy by giving, conquer the liar by truth."[67] Likewise, "Though he should conquer thousand and thousand men in the battlefield, yet he indeed, is the nobler victor who should conquer himself."[68] It is the nature of the Buddhist monks not to resist when they are attacked. There were several incidents in the history to establish this view. Their non-violent behaviour saved many a life. Several Buddhists were persecuted by the Hindu kings, but it was not true of the Buddhist kings. The central teachings of Buddhism throw light on the divine abiding such as loving kindness, compassion, empathetic joy, and equanimity.[69] Patience or forbearance is another important virtue to be cultivated. All these divine abidings are aimed at defusing conflicts arising out of hatred and greed.

The Theravādin, Buddhaghoṣa, writes in the *Visuddhimagga* that one has to undermine the destructive emotions such as hatred and anger. These are the two psychological roots of any conflict. In fact, one's weakness for forbearance and forgiveness is treated as one's strength by Buddhism. Harsh measures against violent actions will only promote violent atmosphere which is not worthy of peaceful life. Harmony is another important Buddhist value. Harmony prevails only when we are able to sort out our differences amicably in any social organisation. Family is not an exception to this rule. All the members of a family may not be united on a particular issue. But some kind of agreement has to be reached so as to keep family ties intact. Similar is the case with any society which is a larger family. At least there are seven important ways by means of which conflicts

67. *Dhammapada*, 223.

68. Ibid., 103.

69. Peter Harvey, *An Introduction to Buddhist Ethics*, p. 243.

can be settled, according to Buddhism. They are as follows: (1) by arriving at consensus on the basis of agreed principles, (2) by majority of voting if consensus fails, (3) by ignoring the monastic offences committed by the guilty which are not remembered by the guilty, (4) by overlooking the apparent offences committed by a person when he committed them due to unsound mind, (5) by setting aside the offences of the guilty when he promises not to repeat them in future, (6) by censuring a monk who admits to committing the offence after cross-examination although he denied it in the beginning, and (7) by covering over with grass. One has to resort to the final method when both the parties fail to reach an agreement. In such an eventuality one monk from each side is expected to acknowledge the shortcomings of each group to show why the groups in question acted in such a way.

It is a well-known fact that non-violence is the catharsis for the Buddha. One's commitment to non-violence elevates him to the highest spiritual level. It is the sole strength of a spiritual person. But violence in self-defence need not be ruled out. A person should not initiate violence, but to protect himself, his family, friends, and his neighbours one can resist it. Subversion of violence, at times, is justified by resisting it. A person, who is not a monk or nun, but guided by the principles of Buddhist morality may resort to self-defence to mitigate violence. He is not guilty of this act for he did not initiate violence. The war against Kaliṅga by the Indian Emperor Aśoka cannot be justified on the Buddhist lines, for his aim was to expand his territory. The war fought by him left thousands dead and disabled although it resulted in victory. This war of attrition affected both the sides. Victory to one person presupposes defeat to the other. Such a situation not only breeds hatred but also animosity which results in avenging the defeat by the loser. As a consequence the people from the both sides remain as the victims of war.

In fact, it was only after the Kaliṅga war Aśoka became a true Buddhist and repented for his expansionist thirst. He, along with his daughter and son, later propagated the Buddhist ideals of peace, kindness, love, and social harmony.

Buddhist concept of non-violence (*ahiṁsā*) is also treated as an ideal way to liberation. It is a positive virtue that establishes harmonious relationships among humans. A violent person destroys everyone including himself, for violence runs down reason. There is no other weapon superior to non-violence in perpetuating the common good. The very survival and continued influence of the Buddhist ethics is largely attributed to its spreading the path of non-violence.

6

Conclusion

To conclude: Buddhism is undoubtedly one of the most influential religions of the world with its emphasis on ethical doctrines. It is not a religion in the sense in which Christianity and Islam are treated as religions. It is a religion *par excellence* in the sense that it is concerned first and foremost with man's spiritual life apart from his social and political life. The Buddhist ethics aims at teaching the individuals how to shape their lives while living in this world. It gives utmost importance to the existential problems faced by the individuals rather than speculative questions. As a result the Buddhist ethics could fit into any society and every political structure. The greatness of Buddhism lies in its ability to make its ethics more realistic and pragmatic. The fundamental doctrines of Buddhism developed over the past 1,000 years. The kind of influence exerted by the Buddhist ethical doctrines is something remarkable. The way in which the Buddhist ideals are followed in Japan, Tibet, Sri Lanka, Thailand, Korea, Burma (Myanmar), and so many other countries is a living testimony to this fact. If the ideals of Buddhism were utopian, there would not have been a large following for these ideals. Although the ethical doctrines ultimately culminate in soteriological goal, their pragmatic value in our day-to-day life is worth mentioning.

The Buddhist ethics aims at self-perfection. In the process not only the individuals gain perfection, but they also benefit the society at large. Self-regarding duties are given utmost importance in Buddhist ethics, for self-perfection is a supreme virtue. In so far as the attainment of self-perfection is concerned a Buddhist has to work out his way on his own. Thus the Buddhist ethics is autonomous. This does not in any way mean it has no concern for society as a whole. As rightly observed by Plato, a just society consists of just individuals. Similarly a perfect society consists of those individuals who attained self-perfection treated as role models by laymen. The society is bound to benefit a lot because of such individuals. But self-perfection is not the beginning and end of Buddhist ethics. One must realise this fact. It is only one side of it. No individual as a social being can be solely interested in his own welfare. He must realise that he is not the only living creature on this earth. Along with him others also have existence in society, both human and sub-human, who are related to him directly or indirectly. The presence of such relations means the presence of social duties or other-regarding virtues. An individual cannot live in a society as a solitary reaper in isolation from others. This is the reason why *saṁgha* is given importance in Buddhism.

The cardinal virtues such as non-injury, non-stealing, keeping oneself away from drinking and other socially unacceptable ways of life will make a society worthy of good life. Sense of tolerance, love, kindness, benevolence, liberality, reverence for elders, and gratitude are some of the greatest virtues advocated by Buddhism for the benefit of individuals and society. Although each individual has to cultivate these virtues on his own, they are applicable to everyone for leading a good life. Another important thing to be noticed in Buddhism is reverence for life. Whether it is human or any other form of life, destroying life in any form is treated as a serious offence by Buddhism. We have already examined this point while dealing with suicide, euthanasia and contraception. The reason why Buddhism banned all sorts of mindless rituals is to contain human and animal sacrifices that were prevalent during the ancient times.

Buddhism advocates that individuals must love others in the sense that one must respect others as one expects others to respect him. One must shed the sense of hatred. Tolerance for others' way of life or living even if the others are not Buddhists is expected of every Buddhist. Similarly one must tolerate injury or pain inflicted on him by others. He must not retaliate against others with same injury or pain. All these virtues are included in benevolence. The doctrine of sympathy and loving kindness necessarily leads us to the consideration of altruistic virtues. Human being as a social being will not be perfect unless he imbibes these other-regarding virtues. Charity, sympathy, empathy, and sharing with others are absolutely necessary to help others and live in the society. You cannot treat the other as your enemy. The feeling of sympathy makes us completely disturbed when others suffer from pain or injury. The first step towards this is to imagine ourselves in that situation. It is called empathy. The great French philosopher Henry Bergson advocated this. Long before him this ideal is seen in the ethics of Buddhism.

Life is dear to everyone. This is a naked truth. We must therefore refrain from hurting others physically or mentally. It is easy to take someone's life, but we cannot get it back for him. Therefore one must control one's anger. This is what we teach our children. In a fit of anger we do things that are unwarranted, and later on we repent for the actions that we committed. An angry person becomes irrational. Therefore, his actions are bound to be irrational. In one of the chapters we discussed the ethical idealism of Buddhism. It is idealism not in the sense that it remains as a mere ideal that is reified. The idealism of Buddhism is something worth pursuing that is highly practical and realistic. In our discussion on the contemporary social issues, we could show how Buddhist ethics helps us in overcoming these issues which are considered to be social evils.

As an ethico-religious philosophy, Buddhism addresses the problem of suffering and how to eradicate it. One's adherence to the Four Noble Truths of the Buddha may bail out one from the bondage and suffering. In the process both the individual and society at large are the beneficiaries for the ethics of Buddhism advanced certain important precepts. The spirit of the first precept of Buddhism made Buddhists all over the world to refrain from killing animals either for pastime or for sacrifice. Indirectly this precept leads to vegetarianism and simple food habits. Although the Buddha openly did not advocate it, it amounts to the same. War involves destruction of human and animal life. Therefore, Buddhism is opposed to war. Every Buddhist must strive to perpetuate peace amidst hatred. Hatred cannot be contained by further hatred. Perhaps war becomes inevitable only when all means to arrive at peace are completely exhausted. Only in such circumstances with a great hesitation a Buddhist might declare war as a weapon of self-defence. Unprovoked violence has to be contained. In the description of *māra*, the personification of evil, the *tathāgata* compares himself to a king who rules his kingdom with righteousness, but being attacked by envious enemies goes out to wage war against them in the interest of his people and kingdom. He who goads others to wage war for righteous cause suffers the consequences of his own evil doing. He would be digging his own pit.

When Buddhist ethics advocates abstinence from theft, its main motto is to develop some sort of contempt for wealth, and the conviction that mere accumulation of wealth does not bring you any happiness. Instead it may lead to misery, for others would be watching your actions closely, and you may be robbed or put to death by others who are greedy like you. Acquiring wealth by hard earned means is different from acquiring it by stealing or cheating others. Whatever one accumulates he cannot enjoy it.

The use of intoxicating drinks was common in India. Under the influence of these drinks, one may lose one's orientation completely and do anything that is detrimental to one's own life as well as for society. In contemporary world we witness people using all sorts of drugs and mescals to gain artificial ecstasy. Under the influence of this mescal or drug they resort to all sorts of anti-social activities. They lose the capacity to think and reflect. Buddhist ethics condemns all such activities for the benefit of individuals. The Buddha as a moral teacher might have drawn these precepts out of his own experience. As an enlightened person he knew what is good and what is bad, what is permanent (*nicca/nitya*) and what is impermanent (*anicca/anitya*). At the same time the aspects related to impermanent world are also dealt with carefully by Buddhist ethics. Its goal may be *nibbāna/nirvāṇa*, but in the process of attaining that goal one may clean up the entire social life of individuals.

Therefore, from the point of view of higher morality, Buddhist ethics offers best solutions to present-day problems faced by individuals in different societies. Of course, no system is foolproof, and no system can guarantee cent per cent success. There are always exceptions. We look for more merits and less demerits in any system. We prefer a particular system because it has more merits. The critics always say that *nibbāna/nirvaṇa* being the final goal of Buddhism it does not have much to offer to society as a whole. It is purely the individual's effort to attain *nibbāna/nirvāṇa*. This may be true, but if every individual practises the precepts of Buddhist ethics in order to attain *nibbāna/nirvāṇa*, then the society in which they live becomes a noble society which is worthy of emulation.

From the social point of view, the views of Buddhism on society, community, primary groups, factors involved in social solidarity, causes for social disorganisation, role of amity (*maitrī*) as a social bond, social change, and leadership are of immense importance to modern society. All these aspects can be derived from the key Buddhist moral precepts. The teachings of the Buddha and his disciples have tremendous social bearing on social and political life of individuals. The Buddhist conception of dynamic reality provides us with greatest insights into the social life of the individuals. In this sense the Buddha was a great precursor to Heraclitus, Marx, Engels, and Bergson. The Buddhist ethics does not have its roots in any dogma or mysticism. In his philanthropic concern for human welfare and the extinction of suffering without any reference to godhead, the Buddha set-up a congenial theoretical base for an egalitarian society.

Bibliography

Primary Sources

Aṅguttara-Nikāya (ed.), R. Morris and E. Hardy, 1885-1900.

Dīgha-Nikāya (ed.), T.W. Rhys Davids and J.E. Carpenter, 1890-1911.

Dhammapada (ed.), S. Sumangala, 1914.

Iti-vuttaka (ed.), E. Windisch, 1890.

Jātaka (ed.), V. Fausböll, London, 1877-96.

Majjhima-Nikāya (ed.), V. Trenckner and Chalmers, 1888-1902.

Samyutta-Nikāya (ed.), S.L. Feer, 1884-98.

Suttanipāta (trans.), V. Fausböll, 1881.

Therāgati (ed.), R. Pischel, 1883.

Vinaya-Piṭaka (ed.), H. Oldenberg, Oxford, 1879-83.

Secondary Sources

Allione, T., *Women of Wisdom*, London: Arkana, 1986.

Aronson, H.B., *Love and Sympathy in Theravāda Buddhism*, Delhi: Motilal Banarsidass, 1980.

Barua, B.M., *A History of Pre-Buddhist Indian Philosophy*, Calcutta: University of Calcutta, 1921.

Batchelor, M. and K. Brown (eds.), *Buddhism and Ecology*, London and New York: Cassell, 1992.

Blackstone, K.R., *Women in the Footsteps of the Buddha: Struggle for Liberation in the Theragāthā*, London: Curzon Press, 1998.

Bodhi, Bhikhu, *The Noble Eightfold Path*, Kandy: Sri Lanka, 1984.

Bunnag, J., *Buddhist Monk, Buddhist layman: A Study of Urban Monastic Organization in Central Thailand*, Cambridge: Cambridge University Press, 1973.

Cabezon, J.I. (ed.), *Buddhism, Sexuality and Gender*, New York: SUNY Press, 1992.

Carmody, D.L., *Women and World Religions*, Englewood Cliffs: N.J., Prentice-Hall, 2nd edn., 1983.

Chapple, K.C., *Non-violence to Animals, Earth, and Self in Asian Traditions*, New York: State University of New York Press, 1993.

Chatterjee, S.C. and D.M. Datta, *An Introduction to Indian Philosophy*, Calcutta: University of Calcutta Press, 1960.

Conze, E., *Buddhism: Its Essence and Development*, New York: Harper & Brothers, 1959.

———, *Buddhist Scriptures* (Anthology of Translations), Harmondsworth: Penguin, 1959.

———, *Buddhist Thought in India*, Ann Arbor: University of Michigan Press, 1967.

———, *Thirty Years of Buddhist Studies: Selected Essays* by E. Conze, Columbia: University of South Carolina Press, 1968.

———, (tr.), *Buddhist Wisdom Books: The Diamond Sūtra and the Heart Sūtra*, New York: Harper & Row, 1972.

Dahlke, Paul, *Buddhism and Its Place in the Mental Life of Mankind*, London: Macmillan and Co., 1927.

Dayal, Har, *The Bodhisattva Doctrine in Buddhist Sanskrit Literature*, London: Routledge and Kegan Paul, 1932.

De Bary, William Theodore (ed.), *The Buddhist Tradition in India, China and Japan*, New York: Vintage Books, 1972.

Demiville, P., *On Buddhist Non-violent Ideals*, Paris: Presses Universitaires de France, 1957.

De Silva and others (eds.), *Ethnic Conflict in Buddhist Societies: Sri Lanka, Thailand, and Burma*, London: West-view Press, 1988.

De Silva, P., *The Search for Buddhist Economics*, Kandy: Buddhist Publication Society, 1975.

Dewaraja, L.S., *The Position of Women in Buddhism*, Kandy: Buddhist Education Society, 1981.

Dharmasiri, G., *Fundamentals of Buddhist Ethics*, California: Golden Leaves Publishing Co., 1989.

Eliot, Charles., *Hinduism and Buddhism*, 3 vols., London: E. Arnold & Co., 1921.

Emmerick, R.E. (tr.), *Suvarṇa-bhāsottama Sūtra*, London: Luzac & Co., 1970.

Eppsteiner, F. (ed.), *The Path of Compassion: Writings on Socially Engaged Buddhism*, Berkeley: Parallax Press, 1987.

Fòrer-Haimendorf, Christoph. von, *Moral and Merit*, Chicago: University of Chicago Press, 1967.

Fu, C.W. and S.A. Wawrytko (eds.), *Buddhist Ethics and Modern Society: An International Symposium*, New York: Green Wood Press, 1991.

Fuji, N., *Buddhism for World Peace*, Tokyo: Bharat Sarvodaya Mitra Sangha, 1980.

Gandhi, M.K. (ed.), *Human Rights: Comments and Interpretations — A Symposium*, London: UNESCO, 1950.

Gard, Richard A., *Mādhyamika Buddhism: Introductory Lectures on Its History and Doctrines*, Bangkok: Mahamukuta University Press, 1956.

Goddard, Dwight (ed.), *A Buddhist Bible: With an Introduction by Huston Smith*, Boston: Beacon Press, 1970.

Gombrich, R.F., *Theravāda Buddhism: A Social History from Ancient Benares to Modern Colombo*, London: Routledge and Kegan Paul, 1988.

Govinda, Lama Anagarika, *The Psychological Attitude of Early Buddhist Philosophy*, London: Rider & Co., 1969.

Guenther, H.V., *Buddhist Philosophy in Theory and Practice*, Baltimore: Penguin Books, 1972.

———, *Tibetan Buddhism without Mystification*, Leiden: E.J. Brill, 1966.

———, *Philosophy and Psychology in Abhidharma*, Lucknow: Buddha Vihara, 1957.

Hakeda, Yashito (tr.), *The Awakening of Faith Attributed to Aśvaghoṣa*, New York: Columbia University Press, 1970.

Hall, R.E. (ed.), *Abortion in a Changing World*, New York and London: Columbia University Press, 1967.

Harris, E.J., *Violence and Disruption in Society: A Study of Other Early Buddhist Texts*, Wheel booklet no. 392/394, Kandy: Buddhist Publication Society, 1994.

Harvey, Peter, *An Introduction to Buddhism: Teachings, History and Practices*, Cambridge: Cambridge University Press, 1990.

———, *An Introduction to Buddhist Ethics*, London: Cambridge University Press, 2000.

———, *The Selfless Mind: Personality, Consciousness, and Nirvana in Early Buddhism*, London: Curzon Press, 1995.

Hiriyanna, M., *The Essentials of Indian Philosophy*, London: George Allen & Unwin, 1932.

———, *Indian Conception of Values*, Mysore: Kavyalaya Publishers, 1975.

———, *Outlines of Indian Philosophy*, London: George Allen & Unwin, 1932.

Hopkins, E.W., *The Religions of India*, Boston: Ginn, 1895.

Horner, I.B., *Women under Primitive Buddhism: Laywomen and Almswomen*, London: Routledge and Kegan Paul, 1930.

———, *The Living Thoughts of Gautama Buddha*, London: Cassell, 1948.

Humphreys, Christmas (ed.), *The Wisdom of Buddhism*, New York: Harper and Row, 1972.

Inada, Kenneth K. (tr.), *Nagārjuna: A Translation of His*

Mūlamādhyamakakārika with an Introductory Essay, Tokyo: The Hokuseido Press, 1970.

Ingram, David, *Critical Theory and Philosophy*, New York: Paragon House, 1990.

Jacobson, N.P., *Buddhism: The Religion of Analysis*, Carbondale: Southern Illinois University Press, 1970.

James, J. and A. James, *Modern Buddhism*, Box Wiltshire, Aukana, 1987.

Jayatilleke, K.N., *Ethics in Buddhist Perspective*, Wheel booklets no. 175-76, Kandy: Buddhist Publication Society, 1972.

Johansson, Rune E.A., *The Psychology of Nirvāṇa*, New York: Doubleday & Co., 1970.

Jones, K., *The Social Face of Buddhism*, London: Wisdom, 1989.

Josey, C.C., *The Psychology of Religion*, New York: Macmillan & Company, 1927.

Kalupahana, D., *Buddhist Philosophy: A Historical Analysis*, Honolulu: University of Hawaii Press, 1976.

Kapleau, Roshi P., *To Cherish All Life: A Buddhist View of Animal Slaughter and Meat Eating*, Rochester (N.Y.): The Zen Centre, 1981.

Keith, A.B., *Buddhist Philosophy in India and Ceylon*, Benares: Chowkhambha, 1963.

Keown, D., *The Nature of Buddhist Ethics*, London: Macmillan, 1992.

———, *Buddhism and Bioethics*, London: Macmillan, 1995.

———, (ed.), *Buddhism and Abortion*, London: Macmillan, 1998.

Keown, D.V., C.S. Prebish and W.R. Husted (eds.), *Buddhism and Human Rights*, London: Curzon Press, 1998.

Kern, H., *Manual of Indian Buddhism*, Strassburg, 1896.

———, (tr.), *The Saddharmapuṇḍarika-Sūtra or the Lotus of the True Law*, Delhi: Motilal Banarsidass, 1968.

Kim, Yong C., *Oriental Thought: An Introduction to the Philosophical and*

Religious Thought of Asia, Springfield, Ill.: Charles C. Thomas, 1973.

Khantipalo, Bhikku, *Banner of the Arhants: Buddhist Monks and Nuns from the Budda's Time Till Now,* Kandy: Buddhist Publication Society, 1979.

Klostermaier, Kalaus K., *Buddhism: A Short Perspective,* Oxford: One World Publications, 2006.

Koller, John M., *Oriental Philosophies,* New York: Charles Scribner's Sons, 1970.

Law, B.C., *Heaven and Hell in Buddhist Perspective,* Delhi: Bharatiya Publishing House, 1973.

Legge, James (tr.), *The Chinese Classics,* Oxford: Clarendon Press, 1893-95.

Lester, R.C., *Theravāda Buddhism in South-East Asia,* Ann Arbor: University of Michigan Press, 1973.

Ling, T.O., *The Buddha: Buddhist Civilization in India and Ceylon,* London: Temple Smith, 1973.

———, *Buddhism, Imperialism and War: Burma and Thailand in Modern History,* London: George Allen & Unwin, 1979.

———, *Buddhist Revival in India: Aspects of the Sociology of Buddhism,* London: Macmillan, 1980.

Mahathera Nyanatiloka, *Guide through the Abhidhamma-Piṭaka,* Kandy: Buddhist Publication Society, 1971.

Max Mòller, F., *The Six Systems of Indian Thought,* London: Longman's, Green & Co, 1928.

McDermott, J.P., *Development in the Early Buddhist Concept of Karma,* New Delhi: Munshiram Manoharlal, 1984.

Misra, G.S.P., *Development of Buddhist Ethics,* New Delhi: Munshiram Manoharlal, 1984.

Moore, Charles (ed.), *The Indian Mind,* Honolulu: University of Hawaii Press, 1967.

Moore, J.H., *Sayings of Buddha*, Oxford: Oxford University Press, 1925.

Mullin, H., *Death and Dying: The Tibetan Tradition*, London: Arkana (tr. Texts with introduction), 1987.

Murcott, S., *The First Buddhist Women: Translations and Commentary on the Theragāthā*, Berkeley: Parallax Press, 1987.

Murty, T.R.V., *The Central Philosophy of Buddhism*, London: George Allen & Unwin, 1955.

Nāṇmoli, Thera, *The Practice of Loving-Kindness: Mettā*, Kandy: Buddhist Publication Society, 1990.

Nananada, Bhikku, *Concept and Reality in Early Buddhist Thought*, Kandy: Buddhist Publication Society, 1971.

Nash, M., *The Golden Road to Modernity*, New York: John Wiley and Sons, 1965.

Nyanaponika, *The Roots of Good and Evil*, Kandy: Buddhist Publication Society, 1978.

Nhat Hanh, Thich et al., *For a Future to be Possible: Commentaries on the Five Wonderful Precepts*, California: Parallax, 1993.

Niwano, N., *A Buddhist Approach to Peace*, Tokyo: Kosei Publishing Co., 1977.

Northrop, F.S.C., *The Meeting of the East and West: An Enquiry Concerning World Understanding*, New York: Macmillan & Co., 1946.

Obeyesekere, Gananath et al. (eds.), *Essays on the Theravada Tradition in India and Ceylon*, Chambersburg (PA): American Academy of Religion, 1972.

Oldenberg, H., *Buddha: His Life, His Doctrine, His Order*, London: Kessinger Publishing, 1882.

Pardue, Peter A., *Buddhism: A Historical Introduction to Buddhist Values and the Social and Political Form They Have Assumed*. New York: Macmillan & Co, 1968.

Paul, D.Y., *Women in Buddhism: Images of the Feminine in Mahayana Tradition*, Berkeley: Asian Humanities Press (translations and discussion), 1979.

Payutto, Bhikkhu P.A., (also known as Phra Rajavaramuni), *Good, Evil and Beyond: Kamma in Buddha's Teachings*. Bangkok: Buddhadhamma Foundation Publications, 1993.

Potter, Karl H., *Presuppositions of India's Philosophies*, Englewood Cliffs, N.J.: Prentice-Hall, 1963.

Puligandla, Ramakrishna, *Fundamentals of Indian Philosophy*, New Delhi: D.K. Printworld (P) Ltd., 1997.

Queen, C.S. and S.B. King (eds.), *Engaged Buddhism: Buddhist Liberation Movements in Asia*, Albany: State University of New York Press, 1996.

Radhakrishnan, S., *Indian Philosophy*, 2 vols., London: George Allen & Unwin, 1923, 1927.

———, *The Dhammapada*, London: Oxford University Press, 1917.

Rahula, Walpola, *What the Buddha Taught*, New York: Grover Press, 1962.

Raju, P.T., *The Structural Depths of Indian Thought*, New Delhi: Asia Publishing House, 1985.

Ramanan, K. Venkata, *Nagarjuna's Philosophy as Presented in the Mahāprajñāpāramita-Śastra*, Delhi: Motilal Banarsidass, 1998.

Rashdall, H., *The Theory of Good and Evil*, Oxford: Oxford University Press, vol. II, 1907.

Ratanakul, P., *Bioethics: An Introduction to the Ethics of Medicine and Life Sciences*, Bangkok: Mahidol University, 1986.

Rhys Davids, C.A.F., *Buddhist Psychology*, London: Luzac & Co., 1924.

Rhys Davids, T.W., *Buddhism*, London: Clarendon Press, 1912.

———, (tr.), *Buddhist Sūtras*, New York: Dover Publications, 1965.

Riepe, Dale, *The Naturalistic Tradition in Indian Thought*, New Delhi: Motilal Banarsidass, 1964.

Rimpoche, Sogyal, *The Tibetan Book of Living and Dying*, London: Ryder, 1992.

Robinson, Joan, *Freedom and Necessity*, Cambridge: George Allen and Unwin, 1999.

Robinson, Richard H., *The Buddhist Religion,* Belmont, California: Dickenson Publishing Co., 1970.

Rouner, L.S. (ed.), *Human Rights and the World Religions,* Notre Dame: University of Indian Press, 1988.

Saddhatissa, H., *Buddhist Ethics: Essence of Buddhism,* London: George Allen & Unwin, 1970.

Saxena, S.K., *Essays on Indian Philosophy,* Honolulu: University of Hawaii Press, 1972.

Sandel, K. (ed.), *Buddhist Perspective of Ecocrisis,* Kandy: Buddhist Publication Society, 1987.

Sangharakshita, Bhikshu, *The Three Jewels: An Introduction to Modern Buddhism,* Garden City, N.Y.: Doubleday & Co., 1970.

Sankrityayan, Rahul et al. (eds.), *Buddhism: The Marxist Approach,* New Delhi: People's Publishing House, 1978.

Sarkar, A.K., *Changing Phases of Buddhist Thought: A Study in the Background of East-West Philosophy,* Patna: Bharati Bhavan, 1968.

Schumacher, E.F., *Small is Beautiful: A Study of Economics as if People Mattered,* London: Blond & Briggs, 1973.

Selbie, W.B., *The Psychology of Religion,* Oxford: Clarendon Press, 1923.

Sharma, Chandradhar, *A Critical Survey of Indian Philosophy,* Delhi: Motilal Banarsidass, 1964.

Sizemore, R.F. and D.K. Swearer (eds.), *Ethics, Wealth and Salvation: A Study in Buddhist Social Ethics,* Columbia: University of South Carolina Press, 1990.

Skolmowski, Henryk, *Dancing Shiva in the Ecological Age,* New Delhi: Clarion Books, 1991.

Stacherbatsky, Th., *The Central Conception of Buddhism,* Calcutta: Sushil Gupta, 1956.

———, *The Conception of Buddhist Nirvāṇa,* The Hague: Mouton & Co., 1965.

Stevens, J., *Lust for Enlightenment: Buddhism and Sex*, Boston and London: Shambhala, 1990.

Stott, D., *A Circle of Protection for the Unborn*, Bristol: Ganesha Press, 1986.

———, *The Conception of Buddhist Nirvāṇa*, The Hague: Mounton & Co., 1965.

Subhuti, Dharmachari, *Buddhism for Today: A Portrait of a New Buddhist Movement*, Shaftesbury: Element Books, 1983.

Suzuki, D.T., *Studies in Laṅkāvatāra Sūtra*, London: Kegan Paul, 1930.

———, *Mysticism: Christian and Buddhist*, New York: Harper and Row, 1971.

———, *Outlines of Mahāyāna Buddhism*, New York: Schoken Books, 1967.

Swearer, D.K., (ed.), *Secrets of the Lotus: Studies in Buddhist Meditation*, New York: Macmillan & Co., 1971.

———, *The Buddhist World of South-East Asia*, New York: State University of New York Press, 1995.

Takakusu, Junjiro, *The Essentials of Buddhist Philosophy*, Wingtsit Chan and Charles A. Moore (eds.), Honolulu: University of Hawaii Press, 1947.

Tambiah, S.J., *Buddhism Betrayed? Religion, Politics and Violence in Sri Lanka*, Chicago: University of Chicago Press, 1992.

Tachibana, Shundo, *Ethics of Buddhism*, Totowa, N.J.: Curzon Press, 1992.

Thera, Narada, *A Manual of Abhidhamma: Abhidhammattha Samgha*, vol. 1, Colombo: Vajirarama, 1956.

———, *The Buddha and His Teachings*, Colombo: Vajirarama, n.d.

Thomas, E.J., *The History of Buddhist Thought*, London: Kegan Paul, 1933.

———, *The Life of Buddha as Legend and Histroy*, London: Kegan Paul, 1927.

Thompson, Kenneth, *Emile Durkheim*, London: Tavistock Publications, 1982.

Tiele, C.P., *Outlines of the History of Religion*, London: Trubner & Company, 1877.

———, *The History of Buddhist Thought*, London: Kegan Paul, 1933.

Upadhyaya, K.N., *Early Buddhism and the Bhagavadgīta*, Delhi: Motilal Banarsidass, 1971.

Valée-Poussin, Louis de la, *The Way to Nirvāṇa*, London: Cambridge University Press, 1954.

Warder, A.K., *Indian Buddhism*, Delhi: Motilal Banarsidass, 1970.

Warren, H.C. (tr.), *Buddhism in Translations*, New York: Atheneum, 1963.

Weber, Max, *The Religion of India: The Sociology of Hinduism and Buddhism*, New York: The Free Press, 1958.

———, *The Sociology of Religion*, Boston: Beacon Press, 1963.

Wijayaratna, M., *Buddhist Monastic Life: According to the Texts of the Theravada Tradition*, Cambridge: Cambridge University Press, 1958.

Wittgenstein, L., *Tractatus Logico-Philosophicus*, D.F. Pears & B.F. McGuinness (tr.), London: Routledge and Kegan Paul, 1961.

Articles

Bartholomeusz, T., "In Defense of Dharma Just-War Ideology in Buddhist Sri Lanka", *Journal of Buddhist Ethics*, 6, 1999, pp. 1-11.

Broido, M.M., "Killing, Lying, Stealing and Adultery: A Problem of Interpretation in the Tantras", in D.S. Lopez (ed.), *Buddhist Hermeneutics*, Honolulu: University of Hawaii Press, 1988.

Cabezon, J.I., "Homosexuality and Buddhism", in Arlene Swidler (ed.), *Homosexuality and World Religions*, Valley Forge: Trinity Press International, 1993, pp. 81-101.

Chapple, K.C., "Non-violence to Animals in Buddhism and Jainism", in *Kraft*, 1992, pp. 49-62.

Edgerton, P., "The Upaniṣads: What do They seek and why?", in *The Journal of American Oriental Society*, 1929.

Florida, R.E., "Buddhist Approaches to Abortion", in *Asian Philosophy* I (1), 1991, pp. 39-50.

———, "Buddhist Approaches to Euthanasia", *Studies in Religion/ Sciences Religieuses*, 22(1), pp. 35-47.

Gosling, D., "Discuss Notes; Buddhism for Peace," *South-East Asian Journal of Social Science*, 12(1), 1984, pp. 59-70.

Hammerli, P., "A Definition from the Viewpoint of a Physician", in G.C. Oosthuizen, H. Shapiro and S.A. Strauss (eds.), *Euthanasia*, Cape Town: Oxford University Press, 1978.

Harris, Ian, "Buddhism and Ecology", in Damien Keown (ed.), *Contemporary Buddhist Ethics*, London: Curzon Press, 2000.

Herdt, G., "Homosexuality", in M. Elied (ed.), *The Enclyclopedia of Religion*, London: Caller Macmillan, vol. VI, 1987.

Inada, K., "A Buddhist Response to the Nature of Human Rights", *Journal of Buddhist Ethics*, 2, 1995, pp. 55-66.

Keown, D., "Are There Human Rights in Buddhism?", *Journal of Buddhist Ethics*, 2, 1995, pp. 3-27.

Ling, T.O., "Buddhist Factors in Population Growth and Control: A Survey based on Thailand and Ceylon", *Population Studies*, 23(1), 1969.

Lipner, J.J., "The Classical Hindu View on Abortion and the Moral Status of the Unborn", in H.G. Coward, J.J. Lipner and K.K. Young (eds.), *Hindu Ethics: Purity, Abortion and Euthanasia*, Delhi: Sri Satguru Publications, 1991.

Nash, J. and M. Nash, "Marriage, Family, and Population Growth in Upper Burma," *Anthropology*, 19, 1963, pp. 251-66.

Rajavaramuni, Phra, "Foundations of Buddhist Social Ethics", in R.F. Sizemore and D.K. Swearer (eds.), *Ethics, Wealth and Salvation: A Study in Buddhist Social Ethics*, Columbia: University of South Carolina Press, 1990.

Ratanakul, P., "Bioethics in Thailand: The Struggle for Buddhist Solutions", *Journal of Medicine and Philosophy*, 13, 1988.

Stott, D., "Buddhadharma and Contemporary Ethics: Some Notes on the Attitude of Tibetan Buddhism to Abortion and Related Procedures", *Religion*, 22, 1992.

Swearer, Donald K., "Thai Buddhism: Two Responses to Modernity", in Bardwell L. Smith (ed.), *Contributions to Asian Studies*, vol. 4, Leiden: E.J. Bill, 1973.

Tambiah, S.J., "Buddhism and This-worldly Activity," *Modern Asian Studies*, 7(1), 1973, pp. 1-20.

Taniguchi, Shoyo, "Biomedical Ethics from Buddhist Perspective", *The Pacific World: Journal of the Institute of the Buddhist Studies*, New Series, no. 3, pp. 75-83.

Venkata, Ramanan K., *Nāgārjuna's Philosophy as Presented in the Mahāprajñāpāramita-Śāstra*, Delhi: Motilal Banarsidass, 1998.

Yuthok, Karma Gelek, "The Five Precepts and the Vajrayana?", *World Fellowship of Buddhist Review*, 32(3), pp. 45-56.

Zwilling, L., "Homosexualtiy as Seen in Indian Buddhist Texts", in J.I. Cabezon (ed.), *Buddhism, Sexuality and Gender*, New York: SUNY Press, 1992, pp. 203-14.

Index